SUSSEX DISASTERS

in the last two centuries

The loss of the Rye lifeboat, the Mary Stanford, see page 81.

W H JOHNSON

S.B. Publications

By the same author
Early Victorian Alfriston
Crime and Disorder in Late Georgian Alfriston
Alfriston Past and Present
Previous Offences – Sussex Crimes and Punishments in the Past
The Kent Murder Casebook
The Macaroni Dancers and Other Stories

First published in 1998 by S B Publications,
c/o 19 Grove Road, Seaford, East Sussex BN25 1TP

ISBN 1 85770 169 0

Typeset by JEM Lewes
Printed by Island Press
3 Cradle Hill Industrial Estate, Seaford, East Sussex BN25 3JE
Telephone: (01323) 490222

Front Cover: (top left)   Remains of the old Chain Pier, Brighton, 1896.
(top right) Vanguard motor accident, Handcross, 1906
(bottom)   The 'Mary Stanford' self-righting lifeboat,
Rye Harbour, 1928

Back Cover: The remains of a luxury caravan, Sunnyside caravan park,
Seaford, after the Great Storm in 1987

CONTENTS

© M.Bensley, 1998

The 'Mary Stanford' Disaster - Rye Harbour, Nov 15th, 1928

INTRODUCTION

I F THERE existed a Beaufort Scale of disasters, Sussex would never register significantly highly. The county has been spared the most brutal and agonising occurrences that befall mankind. Nature here has refrained from committing her most savage acts – not that every disaster can be attributed to natural causes. The county has, nonetheless, its record of grim events. They are saddening, frightening and in some cases profoundly horrifying.

But why bring such disturbing matters to the fore? Because they all form part of the history of Sussex which is not solely about happy, simple folk living out their time against a backcloth of smooth-backed downland, dancing Channel waters, clear skies, beautiful villages and homely towns. Our history, no-one's history, is quite like that. Here, as anywhere else, there are bleak landscapes, darkness and inexplicable outcomes.

Fortunately, we have no legacy of tidal waves; no week-long hurricanes; no volcanoes to ravage us and our times so that the rest of our days are lived out with the taste of fear forever in our mouths. Nor can we record trains with hundreds of passengers plummeting off bridges into swollen rivers; nor aeroplanes, all seats taken, ploughing into mountain sides; no multi-storeyed apartment blocks engulfed in flame. We have had nothing on that scale, for which we may be thankful.

But down the years we have had enough to scar us. Douglas Hurd, Home Secretary, was to describe the storm of 1987 as 'the most widespread night of disaster in south-east England since 1945'. And so it was. But if earlier storms caused less damage – and I exclude that of 1703 when, in addition to whole-sale destruction, 8,000 lives were lost in this country – they resulted in more fatalities, especially at sea. The wreck of *La Nympha Americana* and the loss of the 1809 convoy are examples dealt with in these pages.

I have felt it essential to include the Rye lifeboat sinking, in part as an illustration of the irony which so often attends such calamitous happenings and also because it served to unite the whole nation in an outpouring of sympathy. That same sense of irony is present in the airship accident at Jevington. As with the Rye lifeboat, the dangerous part of the day's work seemed over when catastrophe struck. It is the cruel snatching away of life which heightens the sadness and the awfulness of events like these. This is how it was for the men on the bus which crashed at Handcross all those years ago. They were out enjoying themselves which they did throughout the morning until the last few seconds of their journey.

Some disasters are avoidable. The poor folk in Lewes, submerged in a snowfall, ought to have evacuated their houses. Had they done so they would at least have saved their lives. But they heeded the warnings either too late or not at all. As for the frightful collision of trains in Clayton tunnel, that can only be attributed to a kind of cavalier thoughtlessness.

There is that group of disasters in which no life is lost. Yet I have been struck by the profound sense of loss experienced by so many when the rickety, worn-out Chain Pier at Brighton was finally defeated by the power of the sea. The same deprivation seems to have been felt at Chichester with the collapse of the cathedral's spire and tower. And more recently, the destruction of the great house at Uppark devastated many who were never more than casual visitors. And I am haunted by the old patient at Westhampnett workhouse being carried from the burnt-out building to a horse-drawn omnibus which was to take her from a place she so clearly loved. 'I shall never see the Caroline Ward again,' she called out in her anguish.

It is this loss, this acute and empty feeling, which is the inescapable consequence of disaster. It is present in all of the accounts offered in this book.

W H Johnson
Eastbourne
1998

About the Author

W H 'Johnnie' Johnson first came to Sussex in 1956 and has lived in the county on and off ever since. He was a comprehensive school head for many years before becoming a schools inspector. His principal interest is writing, for which he has been awarded prizes by South East Arts and the Society of Sussex Authors. He lectures extensively on local history and on the origin and meaning of surnames; he also gives prose and poetry readings.

THE SPOILS OF PROVIDENCE

THE WRECK OF *LA NYMPHA AMERICANA*
NOVEMBER 29, 1747

Sussex men that dwell upon the shore
Look out when storms arise and billows roar
Devoutly praying with uplifted hands
That some well-laden ship may strike the sands
To whose rich cargo they may make pretence
And fatten on the spoils of Providence.

ALTHOUGH William Congreve wrote the lines in 1697, they applied just as aptly fifty years and one hundred years later as they had over several preceding centuries. There was a culture of the coast as firmly held in Sussex as in other parts of Britain. The wreck of a ship, so it was believed, was to be welcomed. It was fair game. And if the Sussex wreckers, unlike those in other parts of the country – notably in Cornwall – did not lure ships onto the rocks with false signal lights, they were frequently undeniably callous in their treatment of stricken sailors and passengers. For the spoils of Providence were precious and of more immediate value than the lives of strangers. When men went to strip a wrecked ship – and at times they went in their hundreds – they too often left behind their human sympathies.

If a man could get to the beach fast enough, if he could overcome the waves, if he could beat back others just as anxious as he was to loot, he could perhaps clamber aboard and help himself to any manner of goods. What gifts there were for poor, landless labourers. Why, there might be fine clothing or elegant candlesticks, dainty shoes or dress buckles of silver or gold. And taking these was no theft in the eyes of wreckers, on the look-out for whatever they could use at home or sell. There might be crockery, linen, lanterns or wines; there might be kegs of butter, trunks of personal belongings, barrels of ale, the paltry possessions of some lost sailor or even of some helpless passenger, stranded on the beach, imploring help but cruelly ignored.

A shipwreck, be it caused by foul weather or natural hazards or even by maritime incompetence, offered rich prizes for men who worked as hedgers or ploughmen or day-labourers. The very hint of a shipwreck – perhaps they were warned by the boom of the ship's cannon announcing distress – and they surged from surrounding villages and towns in large numbers.

So down came the poor with the long, hooked poles which they used to haul themselves aboard some storm-tossed vessel, lying half on the beach, half in the still angry waves. Others, less poor, men perhaps deemed respectable, farmers, brewers, tanners among them, came with their horses, their wagons, their teams of helpers, equipped with chains, ropes, sacks and boxes and containers of every kind. They, too, would have their share of whatever was going.

Of course, many of those present at wrecks were involved in smuggling, that common part-time occupation of the poor and the not so poor. These men knew the tides, knew the weather, knew the coast as well as they knew the hidden ways along which to take property which the law of the land would dispute was theirs.

So then, when *La Nympha Americana*, 800 tons, found herself in trouble off the coast of Sussex on November 29, 1747, the crowds were already gathering. The ship, caught in gale-force winds and violent snowstorms as she was beating up the Channel, had made for Pevensey Bay and the shelter of the cliffs at Beachy Head. Her crew, 100 strong, exhausted after a hard day's struggle against the elements, now waited below decks, tossed about in the bowels of the ship by the tumbling sea and praying perhaps that they would be safely beached. Instead, some time before midnight, the ship's bottom was ripped out on the rocks whilst its superstructure was hurled onto the base of the cliffs at Birling Gap.

It was a wretched fate. The *Nympha*, carrying up to sixty guns, had been Spanish-owned only a short time earlier. She had been captured off Cadiz by Commodore George Walker, captain of *The Royal Privateer*. He had brought his prize up through Biscay, had put into Portsmouth, and was now aiming to take her to London with her rich cargo in which he and his crew would have some share.

In addition to superfine velvets, clothes, gold and silver lace, the *Nympha* carried £5,000 in cash, and quicksilver valued at £30,000. Her crew certainly had had much to look forward to. But the storm had changed all that. When the forepart of the *Nympha* crashed against the cliffs, the uppermost section of the hull had broken off like matchwood. Thirty sailors were immediately lost overboard; others struggled to save themselves, either by clinging to what remained of the superstructure or by lowering themselves into the raging waters and attempting to swim ashore. There is no account of how many of these strugglers were lost but certainly some of them drowned.

8

Seaford shags, and others from further afield, plunder the valuable cargo of La Nympha Americana, wrecked at Birling Gap.

Nor could the desperate and terrified men rely on the already assembled landsmen. Indeed, they might already have offered up the old seamen's prayer: 'Oh, God, protect us from the Seaford shags,' a reference to the bird which works the cliffs and rocky shores and seeks its prey among the smaller species of fish. The *Nympha's* crew knew the shags were out there, awaiting the opportunity to begin their work. Some, smugglers for the most part, had passed the hours in a cave known as Parson Darby's Hole, a noted look-out and storage place for men who regularly ran contraband. Yet others had come from the neighbouring villages and, of course, from nearby Seaford. It is scarcely to be credited that in such weather, during a furious, unrelenting storm, with the snow still falling, so many were assembled to plunder the *Nympha*.

But the word was out and they turned up from Bourne, from Sea Houses, from Alfriston, from Jevington, from every hamlet, farmstead and tiny settlement for miles around. And when at last the chance came to board the ship, few made any attempt to come to the aid of the beleaguered mariners. The shags set about their task with a single-minded purpose, wading thigh-deep in the boiling waves, scrambling on to the uncertain and constantly battered shell of the *Nympha* and then lowering themselves down into her innards.

9

On the snow-covered beach, those who had not climbed aboard stripped the corpses of the drowned sailors, or tugged necklaces from the throats of the weak, or ripped from their pockets what paltry possessions they had managed to save. A dead mother and her two small daughters – were they passengers or wreckers? – all three were ignored in the melee. There were other tasks for the crowds. All kinds of booty which was coming ashore, either thrust in by the towering waves or lowered by ropes from the boat, had to be manhandled, carried off, loaded on the backs of horses, stowed in waiting wagons.

At some point the vessel's liquor store was breached and great casks of brandy came on to the beach, and whilst there were those who methodically stacked them to be trundled off in carts, others less mindful of the future broke them open at once. According to the *Sussex Advertiser,* many became intoxicated and perished in the snow. Reports have it that sixty of the looters died of exposure on that raw, wild November day. Elsewhere, a Mr Richardson of Alciston, the reason for his presence unspecified, fell to his death from the cliff top.

Any attempts to stop the hundreds of plunderers failed. The local Comptroller of Customs, Mr Hurdis, and a few others accompanying him, could do nothing to prevent the wholesale looting. The *Advertiser* reports that 'Mr Bouchier, Member for Southwark, part-owner, on the first news of the shipwreck, went down with a warrant from the Secretary of War, for all the soldiers on the coast to assist him.'

That sounds optimistic, 'all the soldiers on the coast', given the foul weather, the slowness of communication, the desperate state of the roads for marching men. But there was some help forthcoming for the Honourable Member, so anxious to preserve the law of the land and his investment. With some assistance from soldiers stationed nearby, Bouchier 'met about twelve smugglers with their loading which they abandoned at the sight of the soldiers but next day returned in great numbers to retake it, on which the soldiers firing, killed two and dispersed the rest'.

Nevertheless, not all of the soldiers fulfilled their duties with such enthusiasm. Some, in fact, took part in the plunder. Three of them were severely whipped at Lewes, charged with having stopped two people and taken from them goods which they had wrongly assumed to be from the wreck. Another soldier was given fifty lashes for going absent without leave after helping himself to a considerable haul of booty.

References to *La Nympha Americana* continued to appear in the *Sussex Advertiser*. On December 24, after another particularly heavy storm, the newspaper reported that 'we are informed that during the two or three first days of last week the goods belonging to the wrecked ship came on shore as thick as

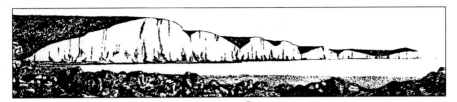

The Seven Sisters, beneath which La Nympha Americana came to grief.

they did at first, and that there was near as many people on the beach ready to receive them. It is supposed that part of the wreck had lodged upon the rock and was since broken, which set the things contained therein a-floating.'

A week later it was reported that 'the bottom of the wrecked ship is found, by which means the owners are pretty certain of recovering the quicksilver'.

On January 4, 1748, the *Advertiser* remarked that 'there have been two loads of quicksilver brought here (to Lewes) which was weighed up from the bottom of the wrecked ship. We are informed that there is a great quantity lies in deeper water and cannot be got up without a diver, for which reason there is one come down from London who proposes to undertake it by the ton weight.'

So the salvage operation went on. According to the newspaper on January 11, 'four more loads of quicksilver were brought to Lewes in the last week'. In the following week about thirty wagon loads were recovered, each valued at something in the order of £800. The bulk of the quicksilver seems to have been brought up too. The cash, £5,000, was also retrieved.

Many profited from the wreck of the *Nympha* in small and in great ways. Few did better than the Lewes watchmaker Thomas Harben, who bought up vast quantities of quicksilver at base metal prices. It enabled him to buy a fine house at Wellingham, near Ringmer, which he dismantled brick by brick and transferred to Seaford where, now known as Corsica Hall, it stands overlooking the sea. Here he settled down to a life of distinct comfort and the exercise of some local political influence.

But the loss of so many lives overshadows all. The dreadful wrecking of *La Nympha Americana* saw the loss of up to at least 100 sailors and wreckers and if tragedies often allow men to demonstrate the nobler side of their natures, it was not the case on this occasion.

A little more than a year later, when the Dutch ship *Amsterdam* went down at Bulverhythe, the mayor of Hastings, William Thorpe, was to write that 'this happening so soon after the *Nympha* has destroyed the morals and honesty of too many of our countrymen for the very people hired to save did little but steal'.

But then, it was the culture of the coast. It had been so for generations and attitudes to wrecks would take yet more time to change.

11

ROMANCE? GLAMOUR?

EXPLOSIONS IN THE SUSSEX GUNPOWDER
INDUSTRY 1764 - 1861

PERHAPS because they were said to manufacture the best gunpowder in Europe – at least, Defoe made this claim on their behalf – the mills at Battle, Crowhurst, Brede and Sedlescombe were permitted to manufacture more than any others in the country. What a tribute. What an acknowledgement to skill. What profits. What a commercial success story.

Perhaps this is the reason for there being more explosions here than anywhere else in the country. Most were in the course of regular testing of the powder's quality. But others, regrettably, were unplanned and had disastrous consequences. There are accounts of several serious explosions in the eighteenth and nineteenth centuries though it would be naive to think there were none earlier in this most dangerous trade. It is reasonable to believe that there was maiming and death and damage to property from the earliest days when, in 1676, John Hammond was first granted a twenty-one year lease on 'four parcels of brookland and upland called Peperengeye Lands in Battle with permission to erect a Powder Mill'. And there is no doubt that, on a monotonously regular scale thereafter, there were violent explosions which caused property damage and even injury and which were never recorded. It is difficult to imagine that everyone in this part of Sussex was reconciled to the ever-present dangers of gunpowder manufacture.

But it is small wonder that the new trade prospered for gunpowder was always in demand. Over the next couple of centuries, where were British soldiers not involved in some or other war? Marlborough's men ranged over the Low Countries; Wolfe's troops fought in Canada; Clive and his sepoys secured vast areas of India; Wellington's men contested Spain and Portugal. And these are just the big names, the major operations, in every child's history book. But there were countless wars, battles, skirmishes. They were fought almost daily on some part of the globe where the flag of Great Britain had been planted or where it was hoped it might be stuck in the ground on a permanent basis. Every day, the product of the powdermills of Battle and the surrounding area was spent in Europe, North America, India, Africa and, of course, on the high seas. And it was constantly replenished from the same modest source.

On the little river Asten there were five mills, each in succession using the same water. The best known of these mills were The Farthing, The House, and Peppering-Eye. Two miles lower down river, at Crowhurst, there were two more mills. Other mills were active at Sedlescombe and Brede where gunpowder manufacture began in the mid-eighteenth century. In each of these places were the various buildings in which the separate processes of manufacture were carried on. Here were the refining houses, where the saltpetre was boiled and crystallised before going to the grinding houses. The grinding of the crystals under giant millstones was overseen by the millmen. Next, in the press rooms, the powder was crushed to thin slabs, said to have resembled slate. From here the wafer-like slabs went to the corning rooms, where a further reshaping into balls took place. These were sent to the sifting rooms where they were graded according to size and purpose. All that now remained was to put the powder in kegs, ready to be sent off by road or barge. And, of course, it was all more complex than this brief description, just as it was infinitely more dangerous than a mere telling can convey.

Thomas Horsfield, writing in 1835, said: 'Next to the Abbey and perhaps its church, Battle is more celebrated for its manufacture of gunpowder than for anything else. The establishment of this dangerous though profitable manufacture is of early date and is now carried on to a very great extent.'

Horsfield seemed satisfied that gunpowder manufacture was not as dangerous as formerly. 'The frequent accidents that have taken place in those celebrated powder mills, it would be harrowing to relate and perhaps uncharitable

An early 19th century lithograph of Battle Powdermill. In 1914 a beam engine was installed to supplement the water power.

to publish,' he wrote. 'Recently, however, they have not been so numerous as they were wont to be.'

It may be useful to look at these complacent assertions. To put the matter in context, perhaps it will be even more useful to look back to before Horsfield's time. In December 1742, Stephen Fuller, writing from Brightling, described in a letter to a relative some especially loud thunderclaps. What he said in such a matter of fact manner reveals to some degree the way in which locals already took explosions for granted. He wrote: 'Our neighbours thought that some powder mills had been blown up and I look upon them to be no bad judges in such a kind of blast, having been more than once alarmed with them by the powder mills in the district.'

The burial register of Battle Abbey contains a harrowing entry, referring to the death of a mill proprietor's sons: '1764 Dec 5 – James Gillimore and Thomas Gillimore buried in one grave, who were accidentally killed by the blowing up of the Sifting House at Sedlescombe Gunpowder Mills; in which house there was computed to be a Ton of Gunpowder; at which time and place there was two other men killed which were buried at Sedlescombe.'

These incidents are not rightly described as accidents; they already merit being called disasters. They are often so ferocious in their effects, so furious in their assaults on men and property that that is how they need to be regarded. The great gunpowder industry was punctuated by disaster after disaster and we can only believe that it survived because it was in the hands of powerful men and because the nation was never-endingly at war. And possibly because the lives of common workmen, who were the most usual casualties, were held less dear than those of the owners.

On July 16, 1787, the *Sussex Weekly Advertiser* gave a graphic report of another accident. 'On Wednesday last between 10 and 11 o'clock in the forenoon, Brede Powdermill belonging to Messrs Brooke, Jenkins and Company, blew up, by which accident two men that were in it at the time were most miserably burnt, one of whom named James Gutsel languished until the next day and then died in great agony, and the other lives with little hope of recovery. The deceased, though he had the presence of mind to strip himself of his clothes immediately after the accident, was scorched from head to foot, and in that miserable condition ran home to his family who lived about a quarter of a mile off. The other in some degree lessened his sufferings by jumping into a pond and extinguishing the fire about him. Had they been at the other side of the Mill, where the powder was running, they must have been blown to atoms. The explosion was felt at Westfield a few miles distant, like the shock of an earthquake. The accident was occasioned by driving a large iron bolt from the troughs. A Powdermill at the same place blew up a few years ago, when one

14

man was blown to pieces, whose limbs were afterwards found scattered a great distance from each other. Another man named Henley was seriously injured at the same time.' The report went on to say that, on this occasion, portions of brick and stone from the buildings were thrown for hundreds of yards. Some years later, a brick from this explosion was discovered, embedded deeply in the trunk of a distant oak tree.

What was probably the worst explosion occurred several years later. The *Advertiser* tells how 'about noon on April 27th, 1798, one of the Battle Powder Mills with a Drying House and Store-room nearly adjoining were blown up with two tremendous explosions and totally destroyed. Three men employed at the Mill were blown into the air and killed. Seven separate buildings were completely destroyed, though only two reports were distinguishable; the quantity of powder exploded exceeded fifteen tons in weight and the damage was estimated at upwards of £5000. A house situate about one hundred yards distant has to be rebuilt while a heavy sandstone from the Mill was carried over the roof of the dwelling and pieces of timber to a large wood half a mile from the Mill.'

An explosion at Brede in March 1808 blew out all the windows in the parish and was heard at Lewes, twenty-five miles away. On this occasion there were three explosions – in the sifting room, in the grinding house and in the magazine which contained 150 barrels of powder.

As ever the *Advertiser* was to give the fullest possible coverage of this dreadful incident in which two workmen and an infant died. 'One of the men named Sinden, at work in the sifting house, had his head and limbs separated from his body and carried in different directions to a neighbouring wood wherein they were collected and placed together and presented a shocking spectacle. The other, named Harrod, it is supposed was killed crossing a small bridge with a barrel to deposit in the magazine, as his left shoulder and part of his head were blown off. The child was killed in an adjacent cottage that was much shattered by the explosion, either by the fall of the chimney or from the stroke of a piece of iron which came into contact with his bowels and tore them out; he nevertheless survived the injury a few hours.'

Poor Sinden was buried at Salehurst and his awful end is recorded in the burial register: 'Cause of death: blown into 5 parts, his head, his leg, thigh and arm, and other arm from sudden explosure of Brede Gunpowder Works.'

The *Advertiser* had not yet finished recording the details of this terrible event. Almost with a sense of wonder at the sheer elemental savagery of what had happened, readers were told that 'by the violence of the explosion, large pieces of timber were forced into the earth and driven to a distance of a quarter of a mile. The town of Battle was strewn with brown paper and some portions of it were picked up at Boreham, distant more than twelve miles, in about fifteen minutes after the magazine exploded.'

What can it have seemed like, paper travelling such a distance, flying through the air, and in so short a time? What can people have thought about such a powerful force on their doorsteps? Twelve miles in about fifteen minutes – who in those days could have credited it? And must it not have made the power of the powder seem so much more alarmingly terrifying?

'The cause of the accident cannot be ascertained,' the *Advertiser* continued. 'Nor is the amount of loss yet known, but some have estimated it as between three and four hundred pounds. An old man named Henley, who thirty years ago received considerable bodily hurt from a similar accident and occupied a wooden building about a stone's cast away from the mill, this time escaped without injury, although the building was shivered about his ears. The unfortunate sufferers have both left widows with families to lament their dreadful catastrophe, and Mrs Sinden who has six children, is far advanced in pregnancy.'

Details aplenty. No causes yet, however. No mention here of safety measures, no reconsideration of working practices.

It must not be thought that no precautions were taken. Near the grinding mills were small changing rooms for the workers. Here, they put on flannel suits and studless shoes, provided by their employers. At the end of the day, before they left for home, the men bathed here, too. Walls in some parts of the buildings had panelled sides and light roofs. Nevertheless, such safety measures were not universally successful as the accounts of accidents demonstrate.

And Mrs Sinden and Mrs Harrod and their families, what of them? Was some collection made to help support them? Were they thrown upon the parish? Did they, could they, sustain themselves? Nobody knows. The mill was rebuilt and continued manufacturing for another twenty years or so.

Nevertheless, mutilations, death, property damage did not deter local historians such as Herbert Blackman from wide-eyed references to 'the romance of the industry'. He is full of admiration for 'the glamour there must be for ever over the simple story of a village enterprise which became an industry of truly national importance'. It was the people in the locality rather than the employees at the powder mills who were nervous, Blackman had been told, as if to suggest that some folk would always find something to worry about. A foreman informed him that the only time he had felt any anxiety was once when powder was being loaded during a thunderstorm. Blackman pointed out that the powder used to go by road on most days from Crowhurst to Battle, with few mishaps. Even longer journeys were undertaken without incident. During the Napoleonic Wars, it was routinely transported by river to Rye and by road to Dartford in 28lb and 56lb kegs.

Blackman, whose handwritten account, *The Story of the Battle Gunpowder Mills*, is dated 1918, had his information from his father and older workers. Indeed, his own grandmother had heard the 1798 explosion and, fearful for her husband's life, had run to the mill with her infant in her arms. Blackman was able, therefore, to draw on first-hand memories of the preceding century. He heard also how, during the Crimean War, the mills had worked night and day. An old van man, Joe Morgan, recounted how he used to take wagon-loads of gunpowder to Tunbridge where they were transferred to barges to be sent to the magazines at Erith.

Whatever occurred, Blackman, whose account is eminently readable, remained in love with the trade which wreaked so much havoc not just on foreign fields but which reached out at regular intervals to damage and destroy much nearer to home. He can, therefore, quite matter-of-factly describe other appalling occasions.

'Sometime betwixt 1850 and 1860, an explosion occurred at the House mills. It was on a Monday morning and the mills were not running as it was customary to dust them down and clean out the beds on which the stones ran. This was done weekly and that morning the foreman, Mr Saxby, had cautioned the millman not to use a hammer but to use a scraper only. However, it was easier to do the work with the hammer and the probability is that he ignored the caution, used the hammer and raised a spark. The force of the explosion that followed was such as to throw him up into the overhead gear with fatal results although the building itself was not greatly damaged.'

Thus, carelessness by a man who was evidently an experienced worker – he was a skilled man rather than a labourer – contributed to his own death. In view of what happened at other explosions, it might almost be concluded that this was a minor incident.

Other serious explosions were described by the ingenuous Blackman. He told how 'a Corning House at Pepper-in-Eye was also the scene of another accident in 1861 when an explosion occurred which fatally injured the man working and destroyed the building'. The building was never again used, its activities passing to those at nearby Crowhurst.

'Near the same scene,' the author continued, 'was another explosion some four years later involving one of the Press buildings. In this instance a portion of the floor was to be renewed. It had been damped and the carpenter was removing some of the flooring when a spark was raised and fitful flashes ran across the floor. These reached the press. There was a terrific report. The carpenter, Chapman, and the millman, Wait, had managed to get outside the building but it did not save them. They both sustained injuries which subsequently proved fatal.'

17

James Morgan, driver of Battle Powdermill's horse-drawn delivery waggon,
pictured in 1918 outside the derelict mill's watch houses when he was ninety-six
years old. The old saltpetre refiring cistern can be seen on the left, and
the small building behind the cistern was the charge room.

Blackman's father, Alfred, a witness to this accident, seems to have possessed the same romantic strain as his son. 'After the explosion,' the old man said, 'I saw the smoke rising and expanding until it looked like a thundercloud in the sunshine of the morning.'

The Sussex gunpowder industry was commercially successful and doubtless it was a significant contributor to the battlefield conquests of British soldiers over two centuries. Nevertheless, in 1874, the Duke of Cleveland, owner of the Battle Abbey estate, influenced by his wife who disliked the trade intensely, refused to renew the lease on the land on which the powder mills stood. At last, they closed down and in consequence, the manufacture of gunpowder moved to Dartford. Thus, an ancient industry, linked to the even older iron industry, passed like its predecessor out of the county. But in the Duke's view, local property had been too frequently damaged and local men too often killed. It was time, he decided, to call an end to a long sequence of disasters.

FOLLOW MY LEADER

THE GREAT CONVOY DISASTER OF DECEMBER 7, 1809

THE convoy of twenty-two ships which set off from Plymouth on Tuesday, December 5, 1809, was bound for the Downs Roads at the eastern end of the Channel. It was no different an operation from hundreds of others in these years. The 186-ton sloop, HMS *Harlequin*, under the command of an experienced young officer, Lieutenant Phillip Anstruther, was to escort the convoy as far as Dover. When she had completed that task, she was under orders to return to Plymouth to pick up yet other eastbound vessels. These, too, she would shepherd through the dangerous waters where French marauders lurked, ready to pick off ships of any nation which had the temerity to trade with Britain.

Napoleon's fleet had been trounced soundly enough over the years and no longer was there any wish to take on the British navy in fully fledged battlelines. The French Emperor's strategy now was to starve his enemy, to strangle her trade, to prevent foreign merchant ships from reaching her shores. The war at sea conducted by the French was now more frequently directed against small trading craft, in a series of relatively minor skirmishes. It was these ships that Lieutenant Anstruther and naval officers like him were deputed to protect.

During the first day's passage up the Channel, with the weather already deteriorating, the ships in the convoy tried to keep as close to their escort as possible. *Harlequin* endeavoured to maintain a regular speed, chivvying both those who raced too far ahead and those who lagged in the rear. The flock was not to stray, especially in the Privateer Passage, the waters after the Isle of Wight where armed French luggers – *chasse marées* – hunted. One of Anstruther's log entries, written on the day of departure, contains a hint of impatience at what he sees as laxness among the convoy members.

'I caused signal guns to be discharged regularly, as handier ships were tending to forge ahead of their allotted station in convoy,' the lieutenant wrote. 'Great difficulty with ships unable to keep station after dark. Some ships are not showing proper lights as instructed.'

Early the next day, Anstruther noted with some relief: 'No sign of chasse maries [sic] so far.' Perhaps they were unwilling to risk a skirmish in the heavy seas.

Doubtless the other skippers were relieved, too. The brigantine *Traveller*, for example, on her way up from Malaga with a cargo of dried fruit and shumack, had already had an eventful few weeks. Since October 26 she had twice been captured by French privateers and twice rescued. Understandably anxious not to be taken again, she now shadowed *Harlequin* closely. Another member of the convoy, the barque *Weymouth*, had also been in French hands on her way from Gibraltar and had been recaptured as recently as November 14, her cargo still intact.

Later that day, Wednesday, December 6, Anstruther recorded: '8 bells in the forenoon watch: Half a gale has got up from the sou'west. Weather showing distinct signs of getting unruly again.'

Whilst they were safe from the enemy for the moment, Anstruther was clearly concerned that his charges should not in the worsening weather lose touch with him.

'4 bells in the afternoon,' the log book records. 'Wind now blowing a full gale from the sou'west with heavy rain squalls. Visibility still very poor. *Harlequin* still ahead of the convoy. Gun fired at intervals to guide ships.'

Below decks, the crew of *Harlequin*, leathery men, tattooed, tarry-pigtailed, sat out the storm. They were accustomed to this. At least, many of them were. Perhaps less confident of their immediate future were the pressed men, those unwilling mariners, the novices, snatched from tavern, from village green, from sea-coast streets, from the very altar rail, and forced to sail before the mast for King George and what they called Liberty.

On the merchantmen, too, the sailors down below were hurled from side to side in their damp, creaking quarters. Their daily conditions were in no way superior to those of the men in the Royal Naval ship. They ate the same hard tack, the same soggy burgoo, the same salted beef; at times, they suffered the same brutal punishments. And when the weather cleared, they would be up on deck in the cruellest of weather, working at the heaviest of chores and ready at the first signal to fend off whoever might be disposed to attack them.

Meanwhile, the seas were in command: the men waited below. Just after midnight, on the morning of Thursday, December 7, Anstruther noted with some satisfaction that 'the storm has abated somewhat but we are having some difficulty keeping the convoy on station now because of fog and sleet'.

The course was now set east sou'east by south. *Harlequin* was still at the head of the convoy. But at some time in that wrenching, wrestling, turbulent night or in the earliest hour of that mist-shrouded morning with its driving sleet, Anstruther estimated his position. And was in error. He was some miles out in his reckoning. And he continued to lead the way.

But now, in the dense, enshrouding fog, the ships could not see each other's lights. Scattered, they were beyond hailing distance. *Harlequin* tried to shepherd them, the muffled reports of her guns giving only the most general indication of her position.

'Estimated entry to Privateer Passage,' the log records at two o'clock in the morning. 'Guns run out. *Harlequin* hauls her wind. Pre-arranged signal fired to indicate new disposition of the convoy.'

Harlequin now took up her position to seaward of the convoy, her flock between her and the shore. There were no French boats there, however. The weather was the sole enemy although Anstruther, confused about his position, did not know that.

It was some time before three o'clock in the morning when Anstruther recorded that the wind, sou'west, was rising to gale force. And here he made his final miscalculation: '(estimate) Beachy Head now due north. *Harlequin* regains position ahead of convoy. Signal guns fired. Pre-arranged alteration of course to nor'east.'

But *Harlequin* was not due south of Beachy Head. She had not yet reached that part of the coast. And she and some members of the convoy following her had turned instead into Seaford Bay, three or four miles to westward. The final entries to Anstruther's log were written shortly after.

'5 Minutes to Morning watch. Wind sou'west abating. Fog. Sleet. *Harlequin* aground. Signal guns fired and flares to warn convoy. We have serious hull damage reports from below mid-ships.'

With which words the log comes to an abrupt end. Anstruther's ship was aground on the steep shingle bank of the longshore drift at Seaford. Fortunately, his firing of the guns had warned off some of the other vessels which had time to change course and escape the danger. But not all them. Some were to share the fate of *Harlequin*.

The situation in which *Harlequin* found herself was perilous. Her back was broken and her stern already sinking. To ease the strain on the foundering craft, the crew was ordered to jettison the guns, all eighteen of them, and to cut away the masts. Consider the sheer enormity of the task: the men on the sloping deck, in a raging storm, manhandling huge cannon, heaving them over the side, while their mates hacked at iron-hard rigging and scarce yielding masts. It is awe-inspiring.

In the turmoil of the seething winter waves no lifeboat could be lowered. The crew, their immediate work completed, made their way to the fo'c'sle, joined by Anstruther's wife and two children, one a babe in arms, the other a two-year-old. Now all that the fifty or so souls, so perilously gathered there, could do was hope.

In the relentless howling of the storm and the fearful thundering of the

HMS Harlequin and her convoy of six merchantmen wrecked in Seaford Bay on the morning of December 7, 1809.

waves, with the sound of the constantly grinding, churning shingle beneath them, those huddled together on the *Harlequin* in the dark of morning neither heard nor saw *Weymouth* crashing on to the unsuspected shallows beyond them at Seaford Head. Here, the ship broke up, her cargo of tobacco, barilla and cork dispersed to the waves, and four of her crew lost. The survivors, six of them, included a cabin boy who came ashore clutching the captain's pet racoon.

Other vessels, blindly following into the raging dark, were to share the plight of the convoy's leader. Half a mile west of Seaford Head, *Traveller*, a small brig, was driven onto the most easterly position on the beach. Her crew was saved though she broke up completely, her cargo lost. The schooner *Albion*, which hauled up not far from *Traveller* and east of *Harlequin*, came on to the beach upright but then the ebbing tide switched her position, causing her to roll over on to her side. The nine crew made for the rigging, lashing themselves to the shrouds and calling out for help, although such cries on such a day were not likely to be heard.

Just west of *Harlequin* was *Unice*. By good fortune, she was not at first so dangerously placed as some of the other craft and her crew of ten and her cargo of cotton, pearl and potash, were saved. *Unice,* however, which had just undergone a £1,000 refit, was totally lost.

The 460-ton Prussian ship *February*, a ship so notably fast that no Frenchman could ever have taken her in these waters, a ship which therefore had little need of convoy protection, was grounded along with the others. Her port side was stove in and the sixteen-strong crew took to the rigging. But now, the savagery of the waves turned her over and all but two of the crew, the mate and a boy, perished. What a brutal irony for such a vessel to end up in this fashion.

Midbedacht, another substantial vessel at 350 tons, from the same German company as *February*, was another ship to founder. The shock of her grounding destroyed her main and mizzen masts and her fore-topmast. Twelve of her crew were drowned; only one survived. It was the weight of her heavy cargo – brandy, wine, sugar, coffee and other miscellaneous merchandise – which contributed to her speedy destruction.

So then, and still before dawn's first light, stretched along the bay were seven of the craft which had set out from Plymouth two days earlier. The men from some of them struggled in the freezing, violent waters; others clung to masts; all were in desperate plight. Five ships lay near *Harlequin* at the east end of the bay. Further east, half a mile or so, was the seventh, *Weymouth*.

The guns fired in distress had roused the inhabitants of Seaford and in huge numbers they flocked to the long stretch of shingle. There, the *Sussex Weekly Advertiser* reported, 'they beheld a spectacle that was truly dreadful, the seven ships being nigh together and complete wrecks, with their remaining crews clinging to different parts of them, imploring that assistance which is natural in such cases'.

The *Advertiser* described the situation of *Harlequin*, 'the decks of which had been blown up and all her masts carried away; she parted towards her midships and all her crew, 46 in number, were crowded on the bowsprit which still remained entire on the forepart of the vessel ... The sea at this time ran mountains high.'

With some ingenuity, the men on *Harlequin* eventually succeeded in lowering over the side a powder cask made fast to a line. The waves took it up and hurled it ashore where it was attached to a hawser. It was then drawn back aboard the ship: there was now a route to safety, a secure line stretched to the beach beyond, down which the endangered sailors might shin to the shingle.

Anstruther's wife and children, however, could not escape in this manner. They were rescued by two men whose enormous courage was apparently matched by their undoubted strength. They rowed out to *Harlequin*, succeeded in clambering aboard, tied the children to their backs and brought them down

Seaford Bay, where six of the ships were wrecked. From a sketch by D N Morgan.

to the rowing boat. The mother was then able to join them although how she came down to safety is not recorded.

Throughout the morning there were several such acts of courage. The sole survivor of *Midbedacht* was saved by Lieutenant Derenzy and men of the 81st Foot from nearby Blatchington barracks. The officer waded into the sea and grabbed the drowning mariner by the hair. The tug of the waves then dragged both men back towards the open water. Another soldier dived in to their rescue. He, too, was soon in difficulty. All three were ultimately saved by a line of soldiers who reached out into the sea to effect the rescue. Such chains of men saved other strugglers in the raging waters that morning.

'Among the saved,' the local newspaper reported, 'was a Sergeant of the 95th regiment or German Rifle Corps who, after being drawn through a tremendous surge by means of a rope, on recovering his legs, appeared only as he would have done after a wet day's march with his sword by his side and his knapsack at his back.'

Yet all was not nobility. Just as sixty years earlier with *Nympha Americana* and *Amsterdam*, more recently with *Brazen*, and with countless similar wrecks down the centuries on this treacherous shore, the looters were out in force. Senior officials of the customs service were horrified at what they witnessed.

'To keep the country people from plundering,' said the *Advertiser*, 'they were under the necessity of requesting the assistance of the Officer Commanding the Dragoons at Blatchington who very readily granted them a party for that purpose.'

But even the rescuers had their belongings stolen. An officer who laid his jacket on the beach returned to find his gold watch missing. The Newhaven Customs Collector, Harrison, who helped to save three men, lost his great coat, his jacket and his boots. Whilst some bundled the wretched survivors up the beach and on to the New Inn – today The Wellington – where they were dried, reclothed and fed, others journeyed back and forth to their homes or to their friends' houses with what they had stolen.

The *Advertiser* stated that it 'found it hard to record the thieving and looting that went on that night, being ashamed to mention that such dastardly acts could have been committed at a time of such bravery, sorrow and heroism'. Even before the dark of night had lifted, there were men on the beach drunk to oblivion. Two men who had broached brandy casks died either from exposure to the foul and freezing weather or from alcohol poisoning. How much like the scene at the wreck of *La Nympha Americana*.

Though many were saved on that grim December morning, the calamitous multiple stranding at Seaford resulted in thirty-one deaths. Their bodies 'are daily washing on shore,' the *Advertiser* reported. 'On Saturday twelve had been picked up, seven of which were carried to Blatchington and five to Seaford.'

As for *Harlequin*, 'there does not remain of her a fragment sufficient to make a coffin for one of the unfortunate survivors'.

And as if to rub it in, on the Saturday after the disaster, a French privateer chased a Greek merchantman almost into the harbour at Seaford. Only after guns were fired from the town and from the barracks at Blatchington did the Frenchman retreat.

A Court of Inquiry was held in the following year. The court decided that no blame attached to Lieutenant Anstruther who was allowed to continue his naval career. It is difficult not to have some sympathy for him. After all, conditions had been appalling and mariners at that time had none of the aids that a ship's captain can now rely upon. Undoubtedly, the court's decision was just.

The Great Convoy Disaster of 1809 is yet another reminder of the perilous nature of the seas off our coast. It serves, too, as prime evidence, were that ever thought necessary, of the dual nature of men and their basest and their noblest qualities and impulses.

IN XANADU

THE COLLAPSE OF THE ANTHAEUM AT HOVE,
AUGUST 30, 1833

THE Anthaeum was not just a vague idea, not simply a wild fancy. It was the fervent dream of an eminent botanist, Henry Phillips, whose aim it was to create a vast, glass dome – it does not seem proper to call it a conservatory though that was to be part of its function – in which the inhabitants of Brighton and Hove would saunter along gravel paths or take their ease in secluded arbours. In this wonderfully light and elegant building, flowers, shrubs and bushes from all over the world and of the lushest growth, would flourish; exotic trees would stretch up towards the skies; alien creepers and the fronds of great palms would offer cover from the summer sun. The overall effect, as in a giant greenhouse, would be soft-shadowed, green-hued. The Anthaeum would attract visitors throughout the year, for in winter furnaces would push out high temperatures, up to 90° to promote the extravagant flora that Phillips was to introduce.

How daring a concept this building was, larger than the domes of St Paul's and of St Peter's, Rome, larger than any dome ever constructed. This was the dream that Phillips took to leading architects, engineers and contractors. It could be done, they told him, assured of the structure's strength and stability from the plans he showed them. It is not difficult to understand their enthusiasm for the scheme. It must have seemed of a part with the adventurous building which had been going ahead in the two towns for the past fifty years.

The local population in the 1830s stood at perhaps 40,000. Brighton was a building boom-town and whilst its slums and artisan housing were squalid, the seafront and its immediate hinterland could boast elegant squares, terraces and circuses, exquisite chapels and churches, fine buildings to match anywhere else in the country. Here were the creations of Barry, Busby and the two Wilds. Just like Decimus Burton at St Leonards and Joseph Kay at Hastings, the architects, builders and contractors of Brighton were adding their imprint to the now fashionable coastline. And Henry Phillips was as ardent as they in his wish to create something fine and lasting. Some years earlier he had espoused a similar plan – the Athenaeum project in Oriental Place in 1825 – although

26

The proposed Athenaeum at Oriental Place, Brighton.

this had come to nothing. But Phillips was undeterred by his previous setback. He had every confidence in The Anthaeum. This project could not fail.

Just north of the coast road and not a couple of hundred yards from East Hove beach, Phillips found a piece of land, some of which comprised a piggery, a gravel pit and a brickyard. He purchased one and a half acres from its owner, the extremely wealthy Isaac Lyon Goldsmid, who also invested in the development. This site, half a mile beyond Brighton's western boundary, lay behind Adelaide Crescent, which was already in existence.

The dome, which according to *The Times* would have formed 'one of the most splendid ornaments in the world,' was at first named the Oriental Garden, a nod in the direction of Phillips' earlier unsuccessful venture. Its name was shortly changed, however, to The Anthaeum, an acknowledgement to the classical world, the Greek word for flower being *anthos*, a fitting enough connection in a town whose most recent successful buildings had owed much to the ancient world.

Springing from the ground as a perfect hemisphere, The Anthaeum was to be 164 feet in diameter and 64 feet high. In order to increase its internal dimensions, there was a plan to sink its floor by several feet. The structure was to be surmounted by a cupola which was to extend its overall height to more than 80 feet. The circumference of this forerunner of the Crystal Palace was 492 feet.

The contractor chosen to provide the massive iron framework was Henry English of the Griffin Foundry in Clerkenwell. He was also responsible for its erection. From the outset, the strong-willed English had insisted that he should be in total charge of all matters relating to the construction and that he should select both the architect and the engineer. Phillips had agreed to this though he was later to regret greatly the power he had handed over to English.

Amon Henry Wilds was selected as architect and the experienced Peter Hollis as engineer. Wilds had a particularly impressive background. He and his father had been responsible for the building of Oriental Place as well as Brunswick Terrace and Brunswick Place and other eminent Brighton landmarks.

Work on the site began on July 29, 1832. George Cheesman, a local builder, started on the deep foundations and the erection of a wall around the base. This work was completed in the following spring. In the meantime, 500 tons of ironwork were brought by sea, the quickest and most economical route, from London to Shoreham. From there, the material was conveyed to the site in wagons, each drawn by twenty horses. Not surprisingly, thousands turned out regularly to watch the wondrous operation.

All went well in the succeeding months: good progress was made. There was constant bustle as the work went forward. Huge, curved iron ribs were sunk vertically, 10 feet deep, into the ground and lodged firmly in solid masonry. Inside and outside the growing dome, men scurried along wooden scaffolding, putting in place and fitting together more and more of the metalwork. Over the months, rings of iron, in sections, were secured horizontally to the ribs, each circle gradually diminishing in circumference as The Anthaeum rose in height. By early summer, after a year of steady labour, the workmen were in the ever-narrowing circle in the upper reaches of the so-elegant building, fitting the last of the cross-beams and spars.

Completion was obviously not far off. No doubt Phillips and the others connected with the project allowed themselves some sense of satisfaction. And no doubt the residents of Brighton and Hove also experienced some sensations of excitement at this most remarkable technological wonder in their midst.

Not that everyone was wholeheartedly in favour of the project. One Brightonian was to castigate The Anthaeum as 'an illusory proposal, hugely and highly dangerous to the public safety. To entrust the stability of a hundred thousand panes of glass, supported by buttresses of cast iron, however enormous, appears to us the height of folly.'

But then, there are always wet blankets.

When the matter of authority and control became a serious problem for the principals in the enterprise, it is not possible to ascertain. Most likely, it had been present as soon as building began. Certainly, by late spring, English and Wilds were at loggerheads but Phillips, who was on site every day, was apparently unable to do anything to resolve matters. The contract which English had demanded yielded all on-site control to him. If Phillips were to intervene in technical disputes, he might face delays; there might even be the possibility of litigation. Goldsmid appears to have played no active part in the project's practical development.

The major dispute, which came to a head in April or May, 1833, concerned the central pillar which might, in the context of The Anthaeum, be likened to a tent pole. Around this pillar there was to be a spiral stairway, leading to the cupola and its observation terrace. Wilds had become anxious when certain pieces of the central pillar failed to arrive. Without its being strengthened, he was certain that it would be unable to fulfil its prime function. By now, however, English was of the view that the pillar was not at all necessary; that the structure would stand without it; that the ribs would be satisfactorily supported on a narrow terracing at the top. The ribs after all were in firm foundations; were of cast iron; had enough surrounding supports to hold them. English scorned Wilds' fears. He insisted that the mutual support of carefully balanced forces would ensure the structure's permanence. Henry Phillips, admittedly no authority on such matters, supported English. For the time being, however, the pillar was left in place.

But the rift between the two men was now too great, Wilds being unable to accept the contractor's sanguine view. He was seriously concerned about the stability of the framework. So virulent was the disagreement between the two men that either Wilds was dismissed or he resigned. In any event, he was forbidden to set foot on the premises again.

Shortly afterwards Peter Hollis left the project for the same reason as Wilds. If the pillar were to come out, he told English, additional braces would be required to strengthen the ribs. Again, English was adamant that he knew what he was doing: whatever decision was arrived at would be his alone. In consequence, for the last three months of the operation, the contractor was without the architect and the engineer he had initially insisted on appointing.

In spite of all of the internal wrangling, the final phase of the building went on apace. It was to be opened to the public on August 29; there was to be a grand official opening on September 1, remarkably a Sunday, which gives some indication of the importance of the occasion. In the meantime, The Anthaeum drew thousands each day to marvel at its delicate strength. A *Brighton Guardian* reporter who visited the site several times in the course of its erection still felt a sense of wonder at its remarkable qualities. His unbounded enthusiasm is evident in one of his reports where he wrote: 'The space seemed immense and on looking at the building as it stood – the largest dome in the world – he (the writer) could not help admiring the boldness of the

29

The Anthaeum from an aquatint of the period.

mind that had projected and the skill of those who had carried into effect this triumph of human art and ingenuity.'

Doubtless many of the visitors anticipated the time when they would be free to spend their leisure time there, to admire the strange plants and trees, to sit perhaps on one of the 800 seats, to take refreshment at one of the kiosks or merely to gaze in wonderment at yet another triumph of the age. Not that entry was to be free. The daily charge – Mondays, Wednesdays, Fridays only – was to be one shilling, whilst the annual subscription for entry on these days was set at a guinea. For two guineas a year, entry was to be allowed every day of the week. Clearly there would be no working men with their families at weekends.

Only days before the projected opening, English had most of the internal scaffolding taken away. It may be that the central pillar was also removed on this occasion although that is uncertain. After a short time, however, the scaffolding was hurriedly replaced and additional ironwork was introduced. There was a distortion of the ribs where they met the terrace of the cupola. Nevertheless, English was undeterred.

In the following days, although some might have felt uneasy about it, the general public were for the first time allowed inside the building. It is unlikely that they were charged entry for some of the scaffolding was still in place. Phillips, anxious now for the first time about the stability of his Anthaeum, had arranged for John Rennie, the celebrated engineer, and Decimus Burton, the founder and builder of St Leonards, to carry out an inspection on Saturday,

30

August 31, the day prior to the official opening.

On the Friday morning, however, when Phillips arrived at The Anthaeum, all of the scaffolding had been taken down. And so had the central pillar.

Who made the decision to leave the building in its unsupported state? Reports vary. Some sources held a foreman responsible. Could it have been so? Surely not. The controlling hand in the construction of The Anthaeum was that of Henry English. It had been so from the beginning. He had appointed and dismissed both Wilds and Hollis; he had retained absolute authority from the start. It is not conceivable that at the last gasp a foreman would take independent action on such a major issue. English undoubtedly reached the decision to remove the scaffolding and the central pillar the previous evening, after the visiting crowds had left. He had dismissed the fears of Wilds and Hollis without any misgivings. Any worries expressed by Phillips – he was only a botanist, after all – were groundless. And why on earth should Rennie and Burton be called in? After all, Rennie built massive docks and harbours and Burton put up grand terraces. But what could they know of airy, delicate structures of cast iron? What could they advise him about when it came to The Anthaeum? Still, they might support Phillips in his groundless fears. So who, then, decided to take down the central pillar? English and no other for he knew that if he did so, no-one could inspect the building. It would be impossible to climb closely enough to those areas about which there was concern. So let there be no finger pointed at some or other hapless foreman for taking a decision which was to prove disastrous. Henry English gave the instructions that all the supports should be taken away, allowing The Anthaeum to be viewed in all its freestanding gracefulness.

Only hours after Phillips' astonished arrival came the crowds, unaware both of the politics of the affair and of the principles of mechanics. In they flocked, entranced and trusting. And with them came the *Guardian* reporter. 'The effect was particularly grand,' he wrote. 'The walks were partly formed and many thousands of plants, some of them extremely curious and rare, covered the walls and mounds of earth, enabling the visitors to judge the effect which would be produced when it was finished.' And of course, when the glass panes were installed the following week, it would all be even more captivating.

But the reporter also happened to notice 'the heavy appearance at the top and the peculiar twist of some of the ribs which had acquired a considerable bend'. He had even mentioned this to the foreman. It was nothing, he was told. There had been some slight error in the ground plan which had thrown out the way in which the ribs met at the top of the dome. But it was nothing to be concerned about.

That Friday evening, after the crowds in their thousands had gone home, only two workmen remained inside The Anthaeum, locking up for the night. At about seven o'clock, just twenty-four hours after the scaffolding and the pillar had been taken down, the men heard a cracking above them. They did not wait. They ran out of the building, cleared a fence and reached safety just as the whole, massive, beautiful dream collapsed. First, the top of the dome came crashing down and then the ribs, 'one after another, like a pack of cards, accompanied by a sound resembling the continued firing of cannon'. How would it have sounded if the 100,000 panes, a whole two acres of glass, had already been in place?

'The millions of sparks produced by so many pieces of iron striking against each other,' said the *Guardian* man, 'made it appear as if the dome had fallen in a bed of flames.'

Some men working in the neighbouring brickyard raised the alarm and within a short time the crowds returned. Phillips was summoned. There, standing amid his wrecked Anthaeum, he was alert enough to give orders that no-one should enter the shattered shell. Just as well. In the night more ribs came crashing down.

Later when it was deemed fit to go in, the *Guardian* reported: 'The ground within is not strewed but actually seems made of iron; there is no walking but upon principals (ribs) and sash bars.'

The bars might be used again, it was thought, but the rest, hundreds of tons of iron, would have to be recast.

'Its destruction,' said the *Guardian*, 'must prove a national loss'.

There was a fault in the design. The ribs were intended to meet in a circle and to be supported at the top of the pillar. But they were not precisely opposite each other. Out of alignment by two or three degrees, instead of being in a circle, they formed an ellipse. Phillips had foreseen his dome as a perfect half sphere supported by a pillar. But the plans had undergone changes, Phillips, until too late, deferring to the expertise of the wrong man. Had the central pillar been retained, The Anthaeum might have been standing today.

Immediately after the collapse of The Anthaeum, there were plans to rebuild it. Goldsmid, English and Hollis – yes, it does seem an unlikely trio – came together to formulate a scheme. There was a meeting at Brighton Town Hall where it was conjectured that a figure of between £2,500 and £10,000 would be required to undertake the rebuilding. A committee under the chairmanship of Charles Augustus Busby, another of Brighton's renowned builders, was asked to draw up a plan.

But in the end, it all came to nothing. There never was another Anthaeum. Its massive, tangled piles of iron, like tortured skeletons, lay where they had fallen for nearly twenty years. Not until 1844 was a start made to use the site,

Palmeira Square, seen at the turn of the century, was built on the Anthaeum site.

with the building of Adelaide Square, and some years later Isaac Goldsmid, by then Lord Palmeira, cleared the land for the square which bears his name.

As for poor, devastated Henry Phillips, ten days after the collapse of his dream, as a consequence of the shock he had suffered, the man who had had such a glorious vision went blind.

So there is no Anthaeum in Hove today, no inspiring structure which it was claimed would be the envy of the world. But sometimes, in an exceptionally dry season, on the lawns of Palmeira Square, the fading outline of what has been called 'the ruins of a Steam Age dream' can be discerned from the air, just the last faint hint of something special.

THE LAST OF BOULDER ROW

THE LEWES AVALANCHE, DECEMBER 27, 1836

THE snow storms that began on Christmas Eve in 1836 were said to be the worst in thirty years. Almost the whole country was affected as the snow fell heavily without ceasing for several days.

At Hull, the snow was accompanied by hurricane force winds. At Wootton Bassett, one hundred stage coach passengers were stranded in two small public houses. The military were called out in the Chatham area to clear roads. From practically every county of England reports were of a paralysed country.

In Brighton, a stableman froze to death in Black Lion Street and a milkman dropped dead on his round from sheer cold. The mail coach from Gloucester arrived hours late, at one o'clock on Boxing Day morning, and at the final stage, the driver and guard had brought the mail bags in carts along the beach. The guard had ultimately collapsed from his exertions and was reported to be near death.

Twenty-six sheep froze to death at Landport in Lewes. Elsewhere in the town, a horse and nineteen sheep suffered similarly. Lewes, in the grip of biting winter, was at a standstill. Only by the river was contact with Newhaven possible.

The diary of Doctor Gideon Mantell reads: 'Christmas Day – a snow storm began last night and has continued through the day and everything is most gloomy and wretched. I returned to my den this evening wet through from walking in snow up to my knees – the fire out – the smoke coming down instead of up.'

Another Lewes man, William Thompson, related that 'the previous night had been cold and gloomy but nothing to indicate the heavy snow that was then impending'. Returning to his house in the centre of the town the following day, he remarked: 'I found the snow had drifted over the front door and on its being opened, it fell inwards and froze so hard and rapidly to the doorpost that for nearly an hour the servants were unable to close the door'.

But the discomforts of Mantell and Thompson were of small consequence. Elsewhere in the town there was cause for infinitely greater alarm. Along the very edge of the Downs, where these come to an abrupt halt on the south-eastern

34

side of Lewes and where they overlook that part of the town called, not inappropriately, Cliffe, high winds had forced the snow into thick drifts, in places twenty feet deep. Almost like a cake icing along the rim of the nearly perpendicular cliff, a continuous wall of snow had appeared within the space of a day and it now overhung the houses in South Street below. Down in Cliffe there were some who were justifiably alarmed by what they could see above them and the threat it seemed to pose. But not all were perturbed. It was nothing to be too worried about, they said. The snow would come down when it was ready to do so. That is what it always did. There was no point in fussing about it.

Fifty years earlier there had been a similarly threatening snow wall in more or less the same location. As the temperature had risen, the snow fell with quite fearsome violence, destroying the buildings in its path below and driving all in its way into the river beyond. But when on Boxing Day, 1836, an old bargeman with a long memory went to Boulder Row, the terrace of working men's houses most obviously in danger, he was ignored, accused of making a fuss. No-one wanted to hear what had happened all those years ago.

Later that day there was a further serious warning. There had been a slight easing of the temperature and in consequence, a mass of snow had fallen into a timber yard at the cliff's foot, completely destroying a shed and scattering its contents for a considerable distance. The owner of the yard, Mr Wille, was concerned not solely for the rest of his property – he was genuinely fearful for the safety of the poor families living in Boulder Row. Robert Hyam, landlord of the nearby Schooner beershop, was equally concerned and both men urged the occupants of the terrace to quit their houses temporarily and seek safety elsewhere. Like the bargeman the previous day, they were largely unsuccessful.

But why would the people not leave their endangered homes? Why not heed the warnings? Did they believe that nothing quite so dramatic ever happened to ordinary folk like them? Was tragedy too grand a theme to have any place in their humdrum lives? Was it that the poor felt there was no alternative but to stay? Or rather was the only alternative the workhouse, that most dreaded of institutions? Were some of the poor occupants of Boulder Row more ready to face the dangers of the snowdrift rather than the cold charity of the workhouse?

Next morning, Tuesday, December 27, in the plain light of day, the huge drift of snow above the houses must have looked even more menacing. There had been some perceptible movement. Cracks of increasing width had appeared in the bulky rampart of snow. Icy slabs, some of considerable size, came tumbling down the cliff face, crashing and breaking into pieces against the very walls of the terrace. The back door of a house was driven open and piles of snow filled the yard. Further along Boulder Row, two young women were alarmed when their bedroom windows were smashed by a sudden snowfall. At last, some of the residents began to take the warnings seriously, hurriedly quitting their homes, carrying with them what they could. A Mr Holman allowed them to store their more precious belongings in his warehouse.

Relatives, friends, neighbours, now persuaded of the imminent danger, tried to encourage others, less convinced, to leave. James Rooke, a fifteen-year-old labourer, called on Mary Taylor, imploring her to come away. At length she yielded. She would come

A contemporary newspaper engraving of the avalanche.

straight away, she told him, as soon as she had collected a shawl for her baby from indoors. It seems that the rest of her eleven children were not present at this time.

Robert Hyam from The Schooner, who had tried so earnestly the previous night to persuade the occupants of the terrace to leave, had returned to his task. He had taken Phoebe Barnden and Maria Bridgman by the arms and tried to pull them away with him but they had strongly resisted him. They were frightened but where would they go, they asked him. Where would poor women like them go in such weather, they asked. Desperate as Hyam was to get the women and their families to leave, he was unable to convince them that they would find shelter elsewhere.

Susan Hayward had come from nearby Firle to spend Christmas with her eighty-two-year-old father, William Geer. She and a boy, John Bridgman, begged the old man to leave his house but he stubbornly refused to move from his fireplace. In his opinion, they were fussing.

All of this urging, begging, pleading, had gone on throughout the early morning hours, up to the very moment that what had been feared finally occurred at a quarter past ten. Yet the avalanche when it came, must, in those first few seconds of its short duration, have seemed sudden, surprising almost.

'A gentleman who witnessed the fall,' the *Sussex Weekly Advertiser* reported, 'described it as a scene of the most awful grandeur. The mass appeared to him to strike the houses first at the base, heaving them upwards and then breaking over them like a gigantic wave to dash them bodily into the road; and when the mist of snow, which then enveloped the spot, cleared off, not a vestige of a habitation was to be seen – there was nothing but an enormous mound of pure white.'

After the first hesitant slippage had come the mass, with a rushing, rumbling, deep throated thunder which had grown in volume, excluding all else, all the common sounds of day. Then came the thuds, the echoing crashes, the collapse of walls as the houses shifted from their foundations and were thrust thirty-five yards and more across the road by tons of falling snow. But in all this deafening torrent of noise – the snapping of timbers, the wrenching of door-frames, the cracking of glass, the grinding roar of houses skidding helplessly off their base – the screams of anguish from inside and outside the houses were perhaps unheard.

And then there was a silence and the kind of stillness that so often accompanies a blanketing fall of snow. Seven houses at the end of the terrace had been totally destroyed. Inside there were fifteen people but whether any could have survived, it was impossible to say. Then the brief silence broke quite suddenly.

'The scene which ensued was heart-rending,' the *Advertiser* reported. 'Children were screaming for their parents and women were rushing through the streets with frantic gestures in search of their offspring while in the midst of all this consternation, men were hastening from all quarters for the purpose of extricating the sufferers.'

This immediate response to the disaster suggests that volunteer rescuers had been assembled in advance: perhaps they had been, for within a short time, 150 men were at work, superintended by local magistrates. They dug in relays; they comforted the injured, the dazed and the anguished who waited uncertainly for news; they offered blankets and hot drinks; and when the dead were brought out they carried the bodies on stretchers to the workhouse to be laid out.

But there was the possibility of further falls. The great ridge of snow above had not been totally diminished. There was still a threatening overhang from the remains of the immense drift. What if, while the rescue work was going forward, there were a second, perhaps even a third avalanche? As a precaution, observers were placed on the brow of the cliff to warn of any further movement.

The first to be brought out of the ruins was young James Rooke. He was alive, suffering from a fractured thigh. But Mary Taylor, that fecund mother, who had been persuaded by him to evacuate but who had slipped back into the house for a shawl just seconds before the avalanche, was dead. The baby for whom she had sought the shawl survived, shielded by his mother's body.

A contemporary drawing of the devastating avalanche

Next came the bodies of fifteen-year-old Joseph Wood, Phoebe Barnden, Maria Bridgman and her eleven-year-old daughter, Mary. That obstinate old man William Geer, who had refused to leave, had been killed by a flying spar of wood as the floor of his house was flung over the road. Later in the day, the body of his daughter Susan was brought out. To the very end she had implored him to seek safety away from Boulder Row.

Young John Bridgman, who had been with Susan Hayward when the snow hit the houses, was discovered alive, lying in a passageway. After several hours, the diggers managed to uncover him but before he could be released, another avalanche buried not only him but also his rescuers. Fortunately there was no loss of life and eventually the boy was dug out. Remarkably, like the others who were rescued from under the snow, he had not found it unduly cold.

Mrs Sherlock with her two grandchildren, one of them only five weeks old, was found on the upper floor of her home, fortunate that the roof had not fallen in. At the inquest she told of how her neighbour, Mrs Potter, had asked her to leave.

'She had been gone about a minute or two when it came over at once pitch dark. We were all flung down. I fell close to the bed and I could feel part of the bedstead come over me. My daughter-in-law (Jane Boaks) fell with her head against the chest of drawers. She moaned very much. After some time the baby moved and cried. I pushed it onto her and said, "Jane, try and give the baby the breast". She said "I've done that for the last time, mother". I, after that, heard the noise of people overhead. I slipped my hand along and took hold of hers and told her to keep up her spirits for I heard the noise of spades above and I was sure they would dig us out. She made no answer but only, screamed. She was dead. I then lay as still as I could till we were dug out.'

In all, eight died in Boulder Row, and there were seven survivors. Doctor Mantell records in his diary: 'Six or seven of my former poor patients perished'. Perhaps it is a small consolation to know that if the avalanche had occurred during the previous night, possibly up to forty people might have lost their lives.

Days later, the town even yet deep in snow, its traffic at a standstill, the consequences and ironies of the calamity were increasingly apparent. William Thompson's account illustrates this: 'A melancholy spectacle still awaited us. The furniture and clothes of the poor sufferers were mixed in utter confusion with broken roofs, black bricks from chimneys and ruined crockery while occasional pieces of cake and plum pudding, intermingled with holly and evergreens, exhibited bitter memorials of the festivities of Christmas.'

The dead were buried at South Malling and their names commemorated on a tablet in the church. Today, set back from the road, and exactly where Boulder Row once stood, are Willeys Cottages, named after the man who had tried so hard to evacuate the residents. But there is a more obvious landmark. It is a public house. It is called The Snowdrop.

A DESOLATE AND UNBEARABLE CITY

THE FALL OF CHICHESTER CATHEDRAL SPIRE
AND TOWER, FEBRUARY 21, 1861

A MAN in Portsmouth, they say, one day in 1861, swinging his telescope first to the west, then out to sea, and then slowly traversing eastwards, finally fixed on the cathedral at Chichester, focusing on its magnificent spire. As well he might for at 277 feet it was always an inspiring sight.

One hundred years later, Nikolaus Pevsner was to write that 'no other English cathedral, not even Lincoln, exerts such a continuous presence on the surrounding countryside and it is the continuity which is the important thing; the spire becomes as invariable and natural as the sky and sea'. And that seems well put, save that on that particular day when the Portsmouth viewer had Chichester's cathedral in his lens, within seconds the spire had disappeared from sight and then parts of the tower crumbled. The landscape, which for centuries had incorporated the spire and tower, underwent a sudden transformation on February 21, 1861. Out went continuous presence; what had been taken for granted, what ages past had regarded as invariable and natural, was no longer there.

The collapse of spires, towers, even churches, is not unknown in Sussex. At Framfield, in 1667, the tower fell and was not replaced for 200 years. At East Grinstead, the church, struck by lightning in 1684, burnt down; 100 years later, the tower collapsed due, according to the Sussex historian Thomas Horsfield, to unskilful workmanship and inferior materials. In their time, churches at Withyham, Cuckfield and Ringmer have suffered similar fates. So have many others.

But Chichester Cathedral is of a different order. It is a noble and majestic building, its fourteenth century spire visible for miles around, from the sea as well as from the downlands and distant fields. Men who sailed the Channel, mariners of many nations who might never have set foot in Sussex, saw it as a welcome landmark, a reassurance. Stagecoach passengers passing through the town; militiamen criss-crossing the county; local ploughmen and shepherds, some of whom never even visited the city, knew it as a constant symbol. Perhaps it is incorrect to say that the Cathedral dominated the city but it fitted in, an expected feature of the landscape. The collapse of the spire on that winter's day was, therefore, of powerful emotional significance to many people.

'If Chichester church-steeple fall,
In England there's no king at all.'

So ran the old local proverb. Nor with Victoria on the throne was it incorrect.

It had been the ambition of Dean Chandler, in the mid-nineteenth century, to carry out extensive renovations in the cathedral. He had wanted to open up the building so that the view from the west end to the east end was no longer obstructed. This would, he believed, lighten the whole character of the place as well as provide additional seating for the congregation. Such radical plans, however, demanded the removal of the Arundel Screen which, in the eighteenth century, had been placed between the two western piers of the nave and which effectively shut off the nave from the choir and the chancel. Inevitably, the organ which was supported by the screen would also have to be moved as would some of the choir stalls. In spite of opposition, the work went ahead although only after the Dean's death. Many regretted the dismantling and the loss of so many beautiful features but the forces of change were irresistible.

In 1859 the Arundel Screen was taken down, its stones carefully numbered and stored in the bell tower. The position of the organ was altered; the old reredos was torn away and some of the choir stalls rearranged. The nave was still separated from the choir and chancel but this time by a screen of lath and plaster. In front of this, in the nave, the services took place; behind, in the choir and chancel, architects and builders carried on with their work. It was at this juncture that the parlous condition of significant parts of the building was revealed.

The old Norman piers which held up the central tower were found to be in danger of falling. Their very core was rotten and it was obvious that their foundations and materials were no longer capable of sustaining the loads which they had borne over the centuries. The renovation work had brought this crisis to light. Now, almost by the day, there appeared long, deep cracks in the piers and arches. Whilst the exterior of the tower and spire looked, to the casual observer at least, to be in as fine trim as ever, internal inspection proved otherwise.

Emergency work was now in hand. New masonry replaced old; cracks were sealed; piers and arches were shored up. But none of these remedial measures were of much use. By 1860, according to one eye-witness, 'old fissures extended themselves into the fresh masonry and new ones made their appearance ... the walling began to bulge towards the end of January 1861, first in the north-west pier and afterwards in the south. Cracks and fissures, some opening and some closing, and the gradual deformation of the arches in the transept walls and elsewhere, indicated that fearful movements were taking place

41

The cathedral as it was before the disaster.

throughout the parts of the wall connected with the western piers.'

On Sunday, February 17, 'the afternoon service was performed in the nave of the cathedral as usual but ... was interrupted by the urgent necessity of shoring up a part of the facing of the south-west pier'.

One wonders at the worshippers' confidence in the state of the building at this stage. It should have been evident – at least, hindsight indicates that it should have been so – that there was now a very real element of danger in their situation as they sat at prayer. Was their faith powerful enough to keep all uncertainty at bay? After all, work in the cathedral on a Sunday must have alerted them to the seriousness of matters.

By evening, the Dean and Chapter had reached the decision that no further services were to be held in the cathedral. Builders only were given access, their task to prop up the tower. Despite the apparent danger, the Monday edition of the local newspaper scorned popular fears and fancies, dismissing 'absurd reports circulating as to the danger of the spire falling'.

Nevertheless, inside the building, while the workmen went about their labours, there was a constant creaking and groaning under the tower. 'On Wednesday,' we are told, 'crushed mortar began to pour from the old fissures, flakes of the facing stone fell and the braces began to bend.'

Perhaps it might have been likened to the effects of a series of minor earth tremors as mortar dribbled down, more gaps appeared across the surfaces, more sagging became visible in the piers and the walls displayed further signs of bulging. On the Wednesday afternoon, a large piece of stonework, weighing about three hundredweight, fell down inside the cathedral with a crash and the builders, fearing the worst, ran outside. They returned later, apparently reassured – though by what is a mystery – that the structure was still sound. They continued working through the evening and some of them into the early hours. In the course of the night, however, there was a storm and the wind rose to gale force. When the tower began to rock, some of the workmen decided that they had had enough and went home; others, with a confidence that astonishes, stayed on, working until three o'clock and then, after a brief visit home, they came back to work at six o'clock.

The aftermath. Rubble from the collapsed spire and tower lie in the sanctuary.

On the Thursday the deterioration of the building was all too obvious. It was too dangerous to go on working inside and the workmen left. Nothing more could be done. The collapse of the spire was inevitable and imminent.

Word was soon out and people came in their hundreds to view the fall. When it happened, 'it fell,' according to one witness, 'perpendicularly into the church, as one telescope tube slides into another, the mass of the tower crumbling beneath it'.

It seems to have fallen so easily. And that is how the observer with his telescope, away in Portsmouth, must have seen it, slipping down silently, to be enclosed within the tower before it fell in its turn.

Another eye-witness gave this graphic account of the event. 'It was twenty five minutes to two when the spire fell. There was no previous notice externally ... I had gone into my back room when I was called out, and I saw the spire and the tower sink softly down as a candle sinks down into the socket. As it went, it quivered a little, and appeared to part in two from the base of the spire upwards to within twenty feet of the top, and that piece fell entire ... as it sank, there was a slight bearing of the spire to the south side; but it came down within its own area. The sound was only like that of stones or coals shot down into the street. I am told that the weight of the falling mass was about 1600 tons.'

So was it a disaster? There were no deaths and, by 1865, the spire had been replaced identically by the Gilbert Scotts. Certainly, had an earlier decision been taken to dismantle the spire, tile by tile, stone by stone, beam by beam, and then rebuild it, no-one would have described that as a disaster. But to see it crumble as it did, to see all that strength and beauty destroyed in seconds, must have been powerfully affecting. The loss of the spire was a kind of emotional disaster to those who knew it well, to those in whose lives it played so significant a part simply by being there.

'One topic engrosses all Chichester,' wrote the formerly sceptical newspaperman. 'Nobody seems to think, certainly nobody cares to talk of anything else. How it had been feared; how it had been declared incredible; how it had come to be regarded as possible; how the hour arrived and the cathedral was deserted, and the streets were filled with hundreds of sad spectators; how, at last, the crash came, and the spire was gone; how the city became desolate and unbearable without it.'

TRAIN IN – TRAIN OUT

THE CLAYTON TUNNEL ACCIDENT, AUGUST 25, 1861

B RIGHTON'S elegant yellow stone station was as busy as it always was on a Sunday, the great travelling day. If the railways had only recently opened up a whole new world to the man in the street, he could only really take advantage of his new opportunities by travelling on a Sunday. For on six days of the week in nearly every profession, trade and occupation men and women were at their workplace. Sunday was the only day of freedom for the majority, provided that the demands of church or chapel did not intrude. So on this Sunday, formally dressed middle-class families jostle with men and women of more modest backgrounds. Solicitors and brewery men nudge clerks, leather-dressers and bird-stuffers; ladies' maids and match-sellers squeeze past milliners and laundry women: the station is a mass of visitors making their way down to the seaside whilst others head for the waiting trains that will take them to London or to any of the stations en route. Three trains stand at their platforms. One, an excursion train from Portsmouth, has picked up no passengers at Brighton. Its late arrival, however, is delaying the departure of the other London-bound trains. The crowds this morning are making for the 8.15am non-stop excursion or for the 8.30am ordinary, the so-called 'Parliamentary stopper'.

Finally, the Assistant Station Master, Charles Legg, resplendent in top hat and frock coat, looks at his watch and gives the signal. And at last, off goes the Portsmouth excursion. None of its passengers will be aware until they reach their destination, London, of the drama which has unfolded behind them and in which their train has inadvertently played a part. In turn and shortly afterwards, the two other trains steam out of Brighton station.

Clayton Tunnel, about five miles up the line from Brighton, is one and a quarter miles long. It is the longest tunnel on the Brighton to Victoria line. At each end of the tunnel is a permanently manned signal box. Three hundred yards from the tunnel's mouth on the south side is a signal which, after it has changed from 'Danger' to 'Clear', the train from Portsmouth passes. Henry Killick comes out of his signal box and waves his white flag in acknowledgement as it goes by. Once it has steamed its way into the tunnel, he returns to his box and telegraphs 'Train in' to his colleague, James Brown, in his signal box at the north end of the tunnel. When the Portsmouth train emerges, Brown will carry out the usual procedure and signal 'Train out' to Killick's box.

Killick, looking down the track to the signal 300 yards away, notices that it still shows 'Clear'. As the Portsmouth train passed it, its wheels ought to have activated the treadle and switched it to 'Danger' so that no following train could come into its zone until it was given the signal to do so. Killick has met this kind of problem before. Only yesterday, the signal failed to function correctly when a train passed by. It had responded when Killick had turned the wheel in his box. This time, however, the wheel refuses to budge the signal. It remains on 'Clear.' And as yet there has been no message from Brown that the Portsmouth train is out of the tunnel. What if another train should suddenly appear from the Brighton direction and there is no warning for it to stop? That signal ought to be at 'Danger'.

And at this instant Henry Killick's worst fears are realised.

The 8.15 train from Brighton is coming round the bend and is only 1,300 yards distant. Should it be as early as this? There ought to be a five-minute interval between trains. Can it have been five minutes since the Portsmouth excursion train disappeared into the tunnel? Killick tugs at the wheel in the hope that he can change the signal and make the train pull up but he can make no headway with it. On comes the train, its speed about thirty miles per hour. It will soon be too late to do anything to stop it. The seconds race by. Still he cannot change the signal. Desperate now, Killick picks up a red flag and runs out onto the platform of his box. He raises his arm, waving the flag to catch the driver's attention but to no effect. The train bustles past him.

Has the driver seen him? Is the Portsmouth train out of the tunnel yet? Brown has not yet telegraphed to say that it is clear. Supposing there has been a breakdown in the tunnel: supposing the Portsmouth train is still in there.

Alarmed, Killick rushes back into the signal box and sends an urgent message up the line to Brown. 'Train in tunnel', it says. He follows it up with 'Is tunnel clear?' He is desperate.

At the north end of the tunnel, just as he receives Killick's message, Brown sees the Portsmouth excursion emerge. He sends a reply to Killick – 'Tunnel clear'. Another little emergency over: they happen all the time. Killick is enormously relieved.

When the 8.30 stopping train hoves into view, everything is under control. There is no cause for any alarm now. Things are back to normal. Killick has no anxieties about any train in the tunnel. The tunnel is clear. Brown has confirmed it. Even the signal which had caused him such concern only minutes earlier has righted itself. It has reacted to the 8.15's passing and now it shows

The extraordinarily castellated north end of Clayton railway tunnel

'Danger' as it ought to. But all is well up ahead and so he pulls off the signal to 'Clear'. As the engine and carriages trundle past him, Killick waves. This time it is a white flag in his hand.

But John Scott, the driver of the earlier 8.15 Brighton excursion train, had caught a last-minute glimpse of Killick's red flag, just as he was passing the signal box. He had not been aware of any problems on the line. After all, the signal had been on 'Clear'. Still, the red flag had been shown. He ought to ease down, come to a halt. He shut off steam and put his engine into reverse. So that his guards in the brake vans knew what action to take, he blew a whistle. His train, with its seventeen well-filled carriages, was 700 yards down the tunnel before he finally brought it to a stop.

Then, in complete contravention of regulations, Scott now decided to back his train away from whatever danger there might be further up the darkness of the tunnel.

The two guards on the 8.30 stopping train from Brighton – the third train to enter Clayton tunnel in the space of minutes – applied the brakes when they heard their driver's warning whistle. Ahead of them, they spotted the red rear lights of the 8.15. But their train, travelling at an estimated forty miles an hour, could not pull up in a short enough distance. In any case, the guards could not act in unison. One of them was in the forward brake car next to the engine, the other in the rear brake car. The engine itself had no brakes.

The 8.30 slithers, grinding along the track, its engine thrust into reverse, howling. The wheels no longer have a grip on the rails and they screech as they approach the red rear lights of the train ahead. It is obvious to the driver and the fireman that they will never pull up in time. Both men hurl themselves out of the engine.

The collision, when it comes, is horrific. It is the worst railway accident yet. There are twenty-one dead and two more will die later. They include a child of eighteen months, a four-year-old, a nine-year-old, and several men and women in their sixties and seventies. There are 175 injured. The injuries of some of the survivors are the most frightful imaginable. The dead, the dying, the obscenely mutilated, lie scattered in the dark night of the tunnel.

The flimsy carriages, each with compartments accommodating up to ten passengers, were reduced to matchwood. The engine had pitched over the last carriage, mounting it and, in the words of one witness, 'had shivered it to fragments'. The rear brake carriage had been barged onto the down line on which a train from Victoria was expected in the next half hour or so.

William Lower, a Brighton bricklayer, described the awfulness of the scene. There was, he said, 'a mingled mass of dead and dying men, women and children buried beneath the heaps of the broken carriages, with the engine and tenders to the top of and pressing down on the whole, the steam and boiling water at the same time pouring over the unhappy people ... the spectacle presented harrowed the feelings of all. The bodies of men, women and children lying together in an almost indistinguishable mass, some, although not dead, being frightfully mutilated and blackened by the pressure, presenting a ghastly appearance, sickening even to those whose duties called them to alleviate their sufferings.'

The scene was like some medieval notion of hell.

'The yells and shrieks of the people were awful,' said a witness who had been in one of the front carriages of the 8.15. 'Not only of those who were injured, but the rest of the passengers of the two trains, whose alarm, increased by the darkness, was intense. People were distracted with terror. We had not any injured beyond contusions in our carriage; but people yelled and shrieked and put up prayers, believing that they should never see daylight again. Their fears increased the actual horror of the situation. They imagined that every moment other trains, either on the up or down lines, would run into them and render their doom certain. For some ten minutes we remained in darkness; then lights were hung up against the sides of the tunnel and the scene that revealed itself was terrifying. There, in the background, I could dimly perceive a heap of carriages more or less in fragments which seemed to have been piled one upon the other. From among this mass, and around it in all directions, you could distinguish people lying, sitting or running to and fro, shrieking and groaning. I never witnessed such a scene in my life.'

'I found myself scrambling over the ruin,' William Lower said. 'The carriage I was in was smashed all to atoms from the back. I had a broken shin. I could not see anything as it was dark but when the lights came on, I found myself on top of the ruins. My wife was covered by the ruins and quite dead when I found her. The engine was standing up a few feet from me and appeared to me to have jumped upon the carriage ... The carriage seemed to have been forced upon its side and was leaning against the engine which seemed to have forced its way under the carriage.'

A Brighton grocer, John Lynn, freed himself from the carriage in which he had been travelling and ran through the murk to the south end of the tunnel. A regular traveller on this train, he was aware that the danger was not over. The brake van was blocking the down line and he knew that the train from London was due shortly.

Once out of the tunnel, he went into Killick's cabin. The signalman told him: 'My mate signalled to me "All clear" but the signal would not act'. Killick told him that he had since telegraphed to Brown to tell him of the accident. What seems obvious now is that neither Killick nor Brown had any means of telegraphing the information either to Brighton or to Hassocks Gate, the station north of the tunnel. Nor dare either of the men leave their boxes. Realising the situation, Lynn set off for Hassocks Gate.

'I then hastened over the Clayton hill, knowing that a down train would be due at Hassocks Gate in the course of fourteen or fifteen minutes. I gave the stationmaster from a distance the signal to stop the train which was done. The down train was just starting from Hassocks Gate, when I held up my hands. This was repeated by the stationmaster and the train stopped.'

As a result of Lynn's action, a message was sent at 9.14 from Hassocks Gate to Brighton which read: 'Clayton tunnel; a block on both lines; send assistance'.

Almost at once a team of men came from Brighton to clear the line. Others were enlisted to assist with the removal of the dead and the dying from that dark and dreadful place. These were taken to Brighton Station where they were laid out. More than 100 of the injured were taken to the Royal Sussex

County Hospital in the town. Here, over the next few days, arms and legs were amputated and the searing scalds, which would scar their bearers for life, were treated as well as medical science could then allow.

Hundreds turned up at Brighton station to discover if it was any of their family, any of their friends, who had been brought there and who now were laid out in the office on tables, boards and trestles. So cruelly disfigured were some of the dead that they could be identified only by their clothing or jewellery or some or other individual physical feature which had not had the skin seared off it or which had not been crushed, twisted or broken beyond all possibilities of recognition.

Back at the signal box on the south side of the tunnel, Henry Killick remained at his post until four o'clock. He had originally intended to work a full twenty-four hour shift right through until eight o'clock on the Monday morning. Presumably someone recognised that he was not fit to work on for such a length of time in view of the accident. Nevertheless, he remained on duty for up to seven hours after the collision. It seems incomprehensible. Was he really operating that signal, turning that wheel, both of which pieces of machinery he must have believed had let him down? Was Killick still communicating with the box at the north end of the tunnel, still signalling 'Train in', 'Train out'? He was. And no-one can have considered that to be in any way remarkable. It seems too that he was quite willing to explain his side of what had occurred. To Lynn, he had mentioned that Brown had sent him a message which seemed to indicate that the tunnel was empty. To another witness, he did not hesitate in saying that the trains had come on him so quickly that he 'did not know what he was about'.

Some who have written about this disaster have suggested that Killick was well on in a twenty-four hour shift when the collision occurred, that he was in consequence tired and unable to cope with an emergency. Not so. Killick had worked the previous day until eight o'clock in the evening. He had then gone home and had returned to duty less than an hour before the collision. So why was this man who had worked in signal boxes for nine years unable to prevent the accident? Did the real cause of the Clayton tunnel disaster lie elsewhere? The inquest, held in Brighton Town Hall and which began there on Monday, August 26, lasted for nine days and was to reveal the reason for what had occurred.

In evidence, Scott told the coroner's jury that by the time he was able to come to a halt, his train, the 8.15, was about 300 yards inside the tunnel. He claimed that the effect of putting it into reverse caused it to jerk back thirty or forty yards. This claim, though it was supported by the fireman and by one of the guards, was strongly contested. John Jackson, a steam engine manufacturer, a passenger on the train, estimated that it was about 600 yards in the tunnel before it stopped and that it had backed about 300 yards before the collision.

Henry Tyler, Government Inspector of Railways for the Board of Trade, a very knowledgeable witness, presented the jury with powerful evidence, too. The train, travelling at thirty miles an hour, had reached the downward gradient. Considering its weight, Tyler argued, this train could not possibly have come to a halt in 300 yards. In his opinion, 700 yards was nearer the mark. Scott must therefore have backed up the tunnel several hundred yards, Tyler said, and had failed to take proper safety precautions in neglecting to send his guard back to the signal box first to ensure that it was safe to do so.

Certainly some responsibility for the crash lies with Scott, driver of the Brighton excursion train. But the coroner's jury found the ultimate fault lay elsewhere. The cause of the accident lay not in the vicinity of the tunnel. The focus of attention was to be directed on Brighton station and on railway working practices.

At the time it was customary to allow a train to depart from the platform five minutes after its predecessor. This time-interval system was the accepted method of control. John Craven, the supervisor at Brighton, explained this to the jury: 'It depends a good deal upon the weather as to what time is allowed between the starting of trains. We give more time in dark weather. We do it every day in London; if we did not, we should never get through our business. It is a matter of judgment.'

Is he hinting that if in bad weather it may be expedient to delay departures by more than five minutes, then in good weather, seconds, minutes even, may be clipped off the intervals between departures?

'On a day such as last Sunday,' Craven went on, 'trains leaving at intervals of five minutes would get two miles apart.'

But not all trains travelled at a uniform speed. It was a very haphazard method. And if on some lines it seemed to work satisfactorily, it ought to have been recognised that all lines were not alike. And the London to Brighton line, which carried 3,000 passengers each day, was distinctly less safe than most with its tunnels, cuttings, and bridges which often obstructed the view of drivers and signalmen.

Several witnesses said that on August 25, three trains set off too close together and at intervals of less than five minutes. Charles Legg, Assistant Station Master, who had flagged away all three, stated that the Portsmouth train departed at 8.22, the Brighton excursion at 8.27 and the stopping train at 8.36. Thus, over a period of fourteen minutes, three trains had left the station, all on the same line. This was perfectly in accordance with regulations, he told the court.

But William Holman, a signalman on duty that day, claimed: 'I never knew three trains to leave the Brighton station at intervals so short'. In his opinion, this was attributable to increased travel. In effect, the urge to increase traffic had not been matched by attention to the safety needs of the travelling public. Another factor was probably that two of the three trains were excursions which had to reach London by 10.30, in accordance with regulations relating to Sunday trains.

Holman, although concerned about the leaving times, did nothing to hold back the trains. He said in court: 'I believed that my superior officer, the (Assistant) Station Master, was responsible for the line and the frequency of starting the trains'. He had not, he told the jury, reported himself for any breach of the rules. Whilst the remark raised a laugh, it did at the same time serve to underline the fact that the time-interval system was being interpreted very loosely.

What seems abundantly clear is that Legg, having sent his trains off, believed that from then on the signalmen would regulate the traffic. But Holman did not and Killick could not.

John Scott, the excursion driver, was uneasy about his setting-off time. 'We started very closely after the other train, more so than I ever remember before.' And his guard, Butcher, replied in answer to questioning: 'To the best of my judgment, the Portsmouth train started two or three minutes before us'.

In court, Killick explained how he had had to deal with a non-functioning signal, a resistant wheel and a misunderstanding with his colleague at the north end of the tunnel at a time when three trains demanded attention. That he had been agitated, he admitted. 'I hardly knew what I was doing,' he said. But he added that he was not alone in being at a loss. 'I do not think the drivers of the three trains knew how near they were to each other.'

In summing up, David Black, the coroner, said that he thought Henry Killick had done his duties as well as circumstances allowed. He might be found guilty of an error of judgment but not of neglect. The jury's view was that both Killick and Brown had, through their misunderstanding, contributed materially to the accident but no action was to be taken against them. In spite of everything, it is clear that the jurors had some real sympathy for the men and the awful plight in which they found themselves.

As for Scott, the coroner said that he ought to have sent his guard back down the line as soon as he had come to a halt. However, in backing the train, he had probably acted for the best, thinking that by doing so he was protecting his passengers. Scott was under the impression that the signal behind him gave his train protection from the rear and believed, therefore, his manoeuvre to be safe. In the coroner's opinion, Scott was not guilty of gross negligence. The jurors concurred in this and although Scott's backing had contributed to the violence of the collision, they expressed some sympathy for him.

Charles Legg, however, who had set off the trains and who had given no particular warnings to the drivers, was found guilty of manslaughter through negligence. The coroner's general conclusion was that the first train, which had come from Portsmouth, left at 8.29; that the second went off at 8.32 and the third at 8.36. Thus, the three trains had left within a period of seven minutes. The time-interval system, inherently dangerous, had been recklessly ignored. Nor was it any defence, said the coroner, for Legg, who had broken the rule, to say that the accident had come about because the signalmen had failed to perform their duties properly.

At Lewes Assizes in the following March, however, the grand jury threw out a Bill of Indictment against Legg. What pressures were there on these men to arrive at such a decision? Were there powerful financial and political influences at play? Those who had invested huge amounts of capital in the new transport system might not favour any adverse court judgment against them. This is, of course, simple speculation and it may be unfair. Nevertheless, the decision not to proceed against Legg after such an appalling accident does raise honest doubts.

The Clayton tunnel accident ought to have convinced all railway companies of the necessity to review their procedures and safety practices. In particular, the dangers of the time-interval system ought to have been apparent and the procedure abandoned at once. Sadly it was not. Before the new and safer system of block-working was introduced, there were to be other devastating accidents. There is a deep obstinacy in some men and in some institutions which can only be overcome by repeated proofs of their folly. Perhaps there is some small consolation in knowing that the directors of the London, Brighton and South Coast Railway agreed to give block-working a fair trial between Brighton and Hassocks Gate even though they were reluctant to do so. They would not, however, commit themselves to extending it. Even then, they had not understood the enormity of what had happened and their responsibility for it.

AT THE END OF THE PIER

THE DESTRUCTION OF BRIGHTON CHAIN PIER, DECEMBER 4, 1896

FOR SALE – BRIGHTON CHAIN PIER
PARTICULARS and FORMS OF TENDER can be obtained
of the Secretary, Brighton Marine Palace and Pier Company,
17 Victoria Street, Westminster.

WHEN the above notice appeared in the *Brighton Herald* at the end of October, 1896, it raised something of a stir. Not that there can have been any real sense of surprise for the future of the pier had been debated for some considerable time. The Marine Palace Company had taken it over in 1891 with no intention of prolonging its life. Indeed, the company's major concern was to build the West Pier which was to be more modern, more in keeping with the times. With a new century just over the horizon, how could people be expected to go on with the old-fashioned and undeniably dilapidated Chain Pier? It had had its day. At least, in the eyes of some that was certainly true. After all, modern man could get about; he could travel to Brighton at week-ends; and even if he was not over-wealthy, he had some cash in his pocket. You couldn't fob off modern man with something as unsophisticated as that old Chain Pier.

But not everyone was of that opinion. Old it might be but the Chain Pier had a powerful hold in the hearts of many Brightonians. They did not wish to lose their pier with its strong links with its past – a raffish, somewhat dubious past, maybe, but one that was colourful and fascinating. The Chain Pier was a link with the old days; it was quaint; it had character; it belonged.

There were several suggestions – it could be sold to the Americans and re-erected somewhere across the Atlantic; it could be demolished; it could be removed somewhere else in England and rebuilt.

Then came a new factor into the equation. In October, the borough engineer made an inspection of the structure. At the far end, 400 yards out to sea, he found the huge timber piles by which it was supported were six feet nine inches out of perpendicular. He declared the pier unsafe and from Sunday, October 9, 1896, after seventy-three years, it was closed.

The Chain Pier in 1838.

Fifty-five years later, and the decaying Chain Pier has been joined by the West Pier (top), completed in 1866, and the Palace Pier which, when this photograph was taken, was under construction. Permission for the new pier was dependent upon demolition of the Chain Pier. In the event, nature beat the wreckers to it.

The *Sussex Daily News* of November 6 carried a letter from 'An Old Woman' whom the paper described as 'a lady high in the social scale of Brighton'. She was deeply concerned for the pier in view the decision of the borough engineer. 'Why not leave it to fall away itself? What harm could it do?' she asked. 'As the waves gradually washed away its ruins, it would only increase the picturesqueness and pathos of its appearance – and its eventual disappearance.'

There is always a dilemma for public men when they are called upon to make radical decisions about subjects which have about them some sentimental aura. So it was with the Chain Pier. Its popularity had, of course, been in decline for the past quarter of a century since the erection of the Aquarium. More recently, since the arrival of the as yet unfinished West Pier, its attractions had waned further for they were especially modest by contrast.

How different it had all seemed in 1823. How wonderful the new structure must have seemed in those days. Its deck, thirteen feet wide and nearly a quarter of a mile long, was supported by chains which hung from four graceful cast-iron towers spaced at intervals of ninety yards. The whole massive construction was supported on huge timbers driven into the sea bed. The chains were carried from the last of the towers and across the road where, after passing through Snelling's Bazaar, they were attached to steel plates weighing three tons. These were sunk into the face of the cliff and set in cement. At the Pier head was the landing-stage, an eighty-feet wide platform of Purbeck stone weighing 200 tons.

The Chain Pier was, with its kiosks and booths, immensely popular from the beginning of its career. It was for so many years one of the great attractions of the town. But it was not simply the first pleasure pier. It had an important practical function, in itself a source of endless fascination for those interested in the comings and goings of the famous and the infamous. In those early days, the boats had come in from and left for Dieppe several times a day, had tied up at the pier's end and disgorged people of quality. There were military bands on hand to greet new arrivals at what was for a brief period Britain's busiest cross-Channel port. The Duke of Clarence – later to be William IV – simply loved the pier. It reminded him of the most beautiful place in the world – 'the deck of a ship'. And where the future monarch came, others followed as they had in earlier years when they had flocked after his brother. The town saw the noblemen of Europe, landed gentry, the substantial professional classes, the military and, according to a newspaper of the time, 'the more notorious Mrs Q with the Marquis of Worcester, and other officers of that crack corps of dandies'. The rich, the extravagant, the outrageous, the louche, the depraved and, it has to be said, the inescapably attractive and compelling personalities of the time came to Brighton and came, as often as not, to admire her Chain Pier, noted for 'the fulness of its symmetry and grace, beautiful in times of calm and strong in times of storm'.

How things had changed by the end of the century. It was evident that something had to be done for the now frail old pier. But what?

Friday, December 4, 1896, was especially stormy, particularly in the afternoon. Fierce Channel winds from the south-west whipped up greater seas than had been seen in years. Huge waves constantly buffeted the pier and it was obvious to spectators that this

The pier in 1896, pictured just a few weeks before it was destroyed.

ceaseless barrage was significantly weakening the already uncertain structure. Still, as darkness fell, old Fogden who for nearly fifty years had been the gatekeeper, walked as ever to the pier's end to light the lamp.

'When the evening closed in yesterday,' the *Sussex Daily News* reported on the Saturday, 'the old Pier was standing much as it had done for the last few months, its ancient glory of paint and polish considerably faded and a distinct aspect of dilapidation about its head and its two seaward clumps of piles, which appeared to have derived a considerable tilt from the violence of the south-western gales, and it looked as if another good shove on that side would settle its business once and for all. As it happened, the attack came from the other side but it was just as effective.'

That effective attack, this time from the south-east, began in the mid-evening, whipping up into what some, with exaggeration, called 'the greatest tempest of them all'. There must have been some expectation of dramatic effects because, despite the ferocity of the storm, there were great crowds present along the sea front that December night, braving the drenching spray from the waves which hurled themselves at the shore and onto the road beyond. Shingle and seaweed were already ankle-deep in certain parts of King's Road, Madeira Road, Marine Parade and Paston Place where the excited crowds were thickly massed. Nevertheless, when, at about half past ten, the Chain Pier was brought down by the relentless battering of the sea, it all occurred so quickly that witnesses seem to have been surprised by its suddenness.

Miss Body, who lived at the foot of the cliff and next to the bazaar through which the chains passed, felt the walls shake. She ran to the window. 'All at once,' she said, 'the light at the end of the Pier disappeared and in a moment the whole thing was demolished.' Others present on the front described the collapse as 'a sound as of houses falling' and 'like a lot of guns going off'.

Near the entrance to the pier, where a small group of people stood in danger of having the massive chains fall on them, a spectator called Wilson heard someone call out 'The old Pier's going'.

'I looked in that direction and saw the middle pile go,' Wilson said. 'It fell in a heap. As it went, the chains sank and disappeared from our view. A moment or so afterwards there was a crackling as of breaking timber and the tower of the first pile fell, as if dragged over by the weight of the chains and the span of the chains connecting it with the land sank right down. The light at the Pier-head remained until the last. After the tower on the first pile had fallen, the light went out almost directly – the fall of the tower and the disappearance of the light were almost simultaneous.'

The tremendous weight of the iron chains brought down the whole structure in a matter of seconds. The towers, wrenched from their foundations, toppled across the sinking deck. Only one was not submerged by the night's end, its chains hanging forlornly in the water. The supporting piles stood up like the ribs of some wrecked and long-abandoned craft. In so short a time was the Chain Pier reduced to the status of a lost ship.

Now the water was strewn with huge weather-worn baulks of timber, half a ton in weight, cast hither and thither at the storm's whim. These, eventually numbered in thousands, crashed onto the beach, smashing whatever fishing boats had not been prudently removed by their owners. Bathing machines, wintering on the beach as usual, were given equally short shrift. Other massive timbers, driven westward by the violence of the waves, came up against the West Pier and, in a final ironic act against its usurper, smashed several of its great supporting columns.

Some years earlier, Brightonians were to say, the Chain Pier would have withstood the storm but they were now to admit with some regret that 'it was on its last legs, poor thing'. There was truth in that. The pier had been neglected in recent years. Nevertheless, its passing was deeply felt by many in the town. 'Drenched Spectator', writing in the Saturday edition of the *Sussex Daily News,* only hours after what he and so many others clearly regarded as a disaster, summed up the place of 'the poor thing' in the hearts of many.

'So good-bye to you, poor old Chain Pier! You have stoutly defied many a savage gale to do its worst and have lived to tell the tale. Our fathers and grandfathers had a word for you, and our children and grandchildren have romped

After the storm – all that is left of the Chain Pier.

over you and under you. Generations of bright lads and lasses have sweethearted in your sunny corners and countless invalids have had reason to thank you. I don't know that you are not immortal in a way, for poets have sung your praises and novelists have written of you as a friend. And you are in the records of Brighton and as long as books about Brighton remain, you will be there. And we have pictures of you, by day, by night, in storm and in sunshine, in summer and in winter, and to multitudes of Brightonians yet unborn you will appeal as a great tradition, a glory to Brighton that has passed from sight but not from memory. And, after all, you have not had a bad innings, and every dog has its day – piers ditto. So farewell, grand old Chain Pier that used to be.'

Those lines were written from the heart and presumably early on the Saturday morning for it caught that day's edition. But while 'Drenched Spectator' was penning his lines others were out and about. Despite the gale which had not yet abated, despite a scene of utter desolation 'such as never before was seen in the town and probably never in any other on the British coast', there were huge crowds to see the damage. Not that they saw much of the Chain Pier save for one uncertainly leaning tower, its chains drooping into the water; the stumps of the supporting piles which from time to time appeared as the waves parted; and the two entrance toll houses. Most of the massive chains which had hung in great loops the length of the pier had fallen into the sea or were hidden under the shingle. There was only one span visible. It ran from one of the toll houses, hanging low across Madeira Road before disappearing into Snelling's Bazaar on its way to the cliff face. For much of the day Madeira Road was shut to traffic as workmen strove to cut the immensely thick iron chains.

The sun shone out of a diamond bright sky for most of that winter's day. Yet the storm-force wind still shrieked and the sea raged, flinging sheets of spray right over the Aquarium and on to the road beyond. At about eleven o'clock in the morning, crowds near the West Pier heard a deep grinding sound. With little warning, a stretch of the deck near the entrance fell away leaving staff at work in one of the offices and the refreshment room cut off. It was a lighter moment, however, for it was obvious that the half dozen or so stranded people were in no danger. Perhaps it gave some wry satisfaction to those who saw the West Pier as in part responsible for the decline of the Chain Pier.

The sense of loss which so deeply affected many people did not deter them from seeking some small share of what the tides threw up. The day has been called 'Wreckers' Saturday' on account of the large numbers who turned out to take home some small keepsake and those others whose purpose was to satisfy those simple demands. So there were relics for sale on stalls set up on capstans. 'Small blocks in commemoration of the old Chain Pier' were offered to crowds anxious for souvenirs. Yet others brought along saws, crowbars, hammers and picks to split timbers and to extract bolts and copper-headed nails. They carried off their booty in their hands, in sacks, barrows and prams. The Sussex man has always been ready to accept gifts from the sea.

In the course of the weekend and over the succeeding days, the timbers which had wreaked so much damage were hauled out of the sea. The sole tower to survive collapsed. All that remained of the once so marvellous attraction left little of itself, nothing but the stumps of the piles which with time and, naturally, with tide gradually eroded. Now, after 100 years, nothing remains of the Chain Pier save a plaque on the wall of the sun terrace of the Aquarium and, further along the seafront, at the Palace Pier, the two surviving toll houses which flank the entrance to the Palace of Fun amusement arcade. In view of their history, this is an eminently appropriate site for them.

What is most striking about the destruction of the Chain Pier is the manner in which local people spoke and wrote of its end. One is continually struck by the way in which the pier was addressed 'old friend', 'poor old thing', as though it were possessed of human qualities. Its familiarity was such that it was a sad parting in the eyes of many Brightonians. It was not just old Fogden, its loyal gatekeeper, who felt the loss keenly, like that of the passing of an old comrade. Many fellow townsfolk experienced a similar sense of personal loss.

'The disappearance was spoken of regretfully,' said the *Sussex Daily News,* 'but a general feeling has found expression that, after all, the famous structure came to no ignoble end. It perished grandly in the storm. It refused to die by inches.'

Perhaps that is a fitting testimonial.

THE END OF A GREAT HOUSE

WESTHAMPNETT WORKHOUSE FIRE, NOVEMBER 3, 1899

A FOUL night – torrential rain, gale-force winds and a road as black as your hat – and Jesse Smith was thinking of nothing more than getting back to Chichester. All he wanted to do was to put the cab away; dry, feed and water the horse; get his wet things off, have a hot drink and go to bed. Taking a fare out to Goodwood was decent enough business when the weather was fine but on a vile November night such as this was, it was rotten work. He couldn't wait to get in the house. Then, when he was just a mile outside the city, on the east side, on the road that comes over from Arundel, he saw the glow. Some place on fire, that much was plain. Only as he came nearer could he make out for certain where it was located. It was at the great old house, Westhampnett Place. A fire there? Why, lives would be at risk, that much was obvious. There were perhaps up to 200 people living in the place, many of them unable to fend for themselves. Perhaps he should go there, lend a hand – and sure as anything, they'd need assistance – but instead he decided that the best thing he could possibly do was to make for Chichester as fast as he could and call out the fire brigade. He took his whip to the horse and urged it on towards the city, whilst behind him the fire danced along the roof of the gracious old mansion.

Westhampnett Place, in part Elizabethan but composed of more recent additions, was a building of distinction, of some nobility. With its great staircase, lofty rooms and painted ceilings, it represented much that was typical of the best of the great houses of the past.

And that is why it may seem odd that on that viciously wild night of November 3, 1899, when Jesse Smith spotted the fire, such a magnificent building was in use as a workhouse.

One of the Dukes of Richmond and Gordon had converted the building so that it might be used as a parish poorhouse. Later, in 1834, when the parish unions were formed, Westhampnett Place served a wide area from Selsey to Singleton, from Fishbourne to Yapton. In 1899, the Board of Guardians were paying an annual rent of £50 to the Duke, it being a condition in the lease that they should be responsible for the repair of any damage.

Westhampnett Place was capable of accommodating up to 250 inmates but on the night in question there were only 115 sleeping in. Of these, about fifty men and nineteen women, described as 'mostly poor people of the feeblest condition', were in the infirmaries. Other poor and dependent people in the neighbourhood attended during the day, employed in the workshops, in return for which they were paid either with small cash amounts or food, clothing or other items of which they were in need.

Even while Jesse Smith was urging his horse back to Chichester that gusting night, the workhouse master, Arthur Moore, was already up and about. He and his wife, the matron, had gone to bed some time after ten o'clock. Both of them were tired as they were short staffed; the porter was on holiday and for several days they had been without a cook and an industrial trainer. Perhaps at about ten thirty – the time is imprecise – they were roused by a crash somewhere upstairs. Had the fierce wind forced open one of the windows? Moore had jumped out of bed and in his nightshirt had made his way up to the third floor. There, in the very centre of the building, under the door of the cook's room, unoccupied for the past week, he saw the flicker of flames. The crash which had wakened him and his wife was the ceiling falling down.

Night nurse Bowen, on her way back from feeding two typhoid cases in the isolation ward, had heard the crash. Near the cook's room, she met Moore who told her to evacuate the building. Bowen hurried along to superintendent nurse Loach's room and roused her from her bed. Together, the two women began the clearing of the female side.

The master, the matron and the nurses were not the only ones to hear the crashing of the ceiling in the cook's room. William Waller, an able-bodied inmate, shared a room with half a dozen young boys.

'I jumps out of bed and gets the boys up,' Waller reported. Leaving the youngsters where they were, he went in search of the master. Waller found him on the second floor. In response to Moore's instructions, Waller led the boys through the men's infirmary and took them to the ground by the recently installed fire-escape at the front of the building. He then returned to help the escape of the women in the infirmary.

Others, too, were involved in the struggle to ensure the safety of the patients in the men's infirmary. Many of the inmates, some of them in their eighties and unsteady on their feet, were terrified of using the fire-escape in the gale-force wind and they had to be helped every step of the way down to the ground. One of the inmates, George Frampton, carried a cripple on his back down the stairs. After helping him down, Frampton went back again to help other old men. He had had no time to dress himself. In fact, in the excitement and urgency of the occasion, he seems not to have noticed this for as he later explained, 'I was running about all night without my boots. Then I got my

The gutted remains of the workhouse, essentially just a shell.

slippers and afterwards the Master gave me this pair of boots.'

After shepherding some of the older men down the escape, Moore appeared for a time in the women's infirmary but he was concerned with other parts of the premises. For instance, he shut down the boiler in case of an explosion. No-one else was capable of doing this. When he was satisfied that the situation in each area was under control, he moved on to where there might be a greater need for him. In spite of what was later said – by Loach, in particular – he was busy and performed his role sensibly.

In the women's infirmary, some of the patients were able to manage on their own and some with minimum assistance. But others presented considerable difficulties to their rescuers. Some were bedfast and, wrapped in blankets, had to be carried down the fire-escape; some were lifted down in chairs; some, fearful, needed to be coaxed, pushed, dragged to the safety of the lawn below. From here, in the fierce wind and driving rain, they were directed to the shelter of the laundry in the Isolation Hospital which was detached from the rest of the buildings.

Waller later told how exhausted he had been by the struggle in the women's infirmary. If another inmate, George Wild, had not come to his aid when he was having trouble with one of the last of the women, 'I should have had to let her fall. I was getting done up,' he said.

It is not difficult to imagine the confusion in the building. There were so many of the inmates incapable of looking after themselves. Moore was to say: 'It was the women who were the most feeble. Undoubtedly, if it had not been for the new staircase, we should not have got the old women down as they were helpless, quite paralysed with fear and quite lost for a little while.' At one point, a Mrs White was unaccounted for when a head-count was taken outside. Had she been forgotten? Was she locked somewhere in the building? Had she already succumbed to smoke inhalation? No, quite suddenly there she was, holding up her hand. Yes, she had come down the fire-escape. And confused, had wandered.

There was one casualty that night. Thomas Gilbert, a seventy-two year old, who suffered from asthma, dropsy and heart disease, was seen by the master 'toddling along' with the aid of a stick. Moore recalled calling out to him, encouraging the old man on his way. But then, Gilbert had collapsed and died, a verdict later stating that he had 'succumbed to fright'.

When he was sure that all 115 patients were clear of the building, the master sought brandy, blankets and clothing for the cold and anxious inmates waiting in the Isolation Hospital.

Some outside help eventually turned up. Half a dozen farm labourers from nearby Church Cottages braved the storm. Then, at about eleven-thirty, the fire-engine from Chichester arrived, pulled by Jesse Smith's horse which had been immediately pressed into service when it reached the city with news of the fire. Accompanying the firemen were several men who had been attending a dinner in Chichester and the workhouse doctor, Bostock.

By now, although the fire had a good hold of the roof, its progress was slow and there were strong hopes that the main building would be saved. The master had made no attempt to fight the fire as there was no-one else on the premises he could call on to help him do so. Inmates' safety was his major concern. He, his wife and the three nurses, helped by half a dozen inmates, were totally occupied with the evacuation. In any case, the blaze, being confined to the roof area, endangered nobody. Now, as the bewildered and half-dressed inmates huddled together in the safety of the Isolation Hospital, the master led the firemen to the second floor hydrant, one of several in the building. Each of these was connected to the water tank which in turn was fed from a well in the grounds. But the water pressure was not strong enough so water had to be pumped from the tank by hand. The Chichester volunteers worked the pumps for two hours to a chant of 'Chi! Chi! Chi! That's our war cry!' But it was all too slow to arrest the progress of the flames. Finally, the well, which allegedly held 4,000 gallons, ran dry. What an irony to reflect that in the previous year, the Guardians had decided, in the interest of ratepayers, not to connect the water supply to the mains.

The struggle against the fire was hopeless. Certainly, had the water supply been adequate, the flames could have been beaten but by three o'clock any attempt to conquer them had been given up. The storm still raged furiously. 'I have never had such a rough experience,' said Captain Budden, the senior fire brigade officer. 'It was truly an awful night for besides the heavy rain, there was a gale, a terrific sou'wester.'

As the night wore on, the inmates were taken away to other accommodation in hired horse-drawn omnibuses and vans. Budden recalled the wretched scene. 'It was a sorrowful sight to see the poor creatures being carried to conveyances. One of the women was saying "I shall never see the Caroline Ward again".' Very evidently some had a sincere affection for Westhampnett Place. These bewildered and vulnerable men and women, shocked to be so suddenly wrenched from what were to many of them familiar surroundings, were separated from friends, too. Fifty-five were taken off to the workhouse at Chichester and the two cholera cases to the Isolation Hospital in the city. Another twenty-seven were sent to Graylingwell Mind Hospital. Twenty-three stayed on temporarily at Westhampnett, housed in the Isolation Hospital.

The fire, fanned by the wind, continued to burn until eight o'clock in the morning by which time all that remained was a smoking, blackened ruin. The main building, the core of the once fine house, was gutted. Both east and west wings had been engulfed and the massive roof had fallen in. The detached buildings, including the board room, the laundry, the male tramp ward, the workshops and the stables were untouched. The only parts of the main building to escape were the master's quarters – his dining room, sitting room, bedrooms and office – which had been favoured by the wind direction. Whilst he had lost much personal property, the greater part of his furniture was not affected.

On the Saturday morning, only hours after the fire had spent itself, the Guardians were summoned to a meeting in the West Street offices of the clerk, Sir Robert George Raper. The situation was reviewed. The master gave a report; enquiries were made about the arrangements for the inmates and the meeting concluded with a vote of thanks to Dr Bostock, the Moores, the nurses and all others who had helped.

By November 10, however, when the Guardians met again, the mood had changed. What now perturbed the Guardians was a 'gross insult' which had been directed at the Moores by superintendent nurse Loach. Anxious to uphold the authority and dignity of the superior officers, they suspended the nurse until such time as the Local Government Board had had time to investigate the cause of the fire and the management of the workhouse.

The Local Government Board met on December 4. The meeting and its outcome make for sad reading. After the selflessness displayed by the workhouse staff on the night of the fire, there were now bitter recriminations. It is evident that nurses Loach and Bowen, who had lost personal property in the fire, were resentful of the fact that much of the Moores' property had been saved.

Nurse Bowen was quoted in the local newspaper as saying, 'Did I save my things? Oh no! My room was in the male division and was soon a mass of flame and I could not save anything, not even my bonnet and cloak. You see these slippers? They are large men's boots and I had to borrow them. The Superintendent Nurse is wearing a pair of boots belonging to a patient.'

Perhaps, too, the nurses were not insured for loss as family man Moore had been. Even so, while Moore received £90 from the insurance company – the maximum for which he was covered – he had lost more than that. But the nurses had lost practically everything and this certainly embittered them.

On the Monday after the fire, the local newspaper had carried a full report. After Loach had read the account which lauded the part played by the master and his wife – 'their efficiency was never put to a more severe test than on Friday night and since; it has well stood the ordeal' – she had stormed into the master's quarters, calling Moore and his wife 'the biggest pair of liars' and saying that she would 'make Chichester blaze with it'. She accused the Moores of doing nothing during the evacuation except save their own belongings. Loach claimed that the only time she saw the master was in the Isolation Hospital, reassuring his wife that their belongings were safe, even the children's toys. This was untrue, unfair and unseemly and the Local Government Board's officials deemed it to be so.

The enquiry focussed upon the master's competence both on the night of the fire and throughout his two and a half year tenure. It is not difficult to feel sympathy for him, given the circumstances.

The wonder is that the workhouse functioned as successfully as it seems to have done. And a further wonder is that all of the inmates were brought out of the blazing building and then cared for so effectively by so few people. Undoubtedly, the evacuation of the building, completed within twenty minutes, was remarkable, considering the condition of many of the 115 inmates and the few staff available. Had the fire escape not been installed the previous year perhaps the outcome might have been more serious.

For some weeks, twenty-three inmates stayed on at Westhampnett in the Isolation Hospital but eventually they were transferred to the workhouse at Chichester. Westhampnett did not reopen as a workhouse. Grossly underinsured, it could not be rebuilt.

Nurse Loach handed in her resignation and it is not known where she went. The other nurses, Reed and Bowen, found posts elsewhere.

The board had failed seriously in underinsuring the workhouse. In such embarrassing circumstances, there seems always to be some necessity to find a scapegoat. In this case, Dr Bostock was asked to resign. Asked about the workhouse water supply, Bostock had accepted that he was responsible for this, at least as far as sanitary purposes were concerned. He was unaware, he admitted, that the tank had a capacity of no more than 4,000 gallons and had never realised that if there were a fire there might be difficulties. What an obvious man to take the blame. When he refused to hand in his resignation, he was removed by formal order of the Local Government Board.

The Moores found positions as master and matron at Horsham Workhouse. They left Westhampnett with a testimonial to their good work. In addition to the £90 they had received from the Sun Insurance Company, the grateful Guardians gave them an extra £30 to cover the remainder of their lost property and an additional gratuity of £100.

If there is any deep sadness about the end of this great house, it would seem to lie not in its changed role as a workhouse, nor in its disastrous fire, but in the squabbles that were revealed after it lay in ruins.

A DAY OUT

THE BUS CRASH AT HANDCROSS, JULY 12, 1906

T HERE were thirty-four in the party, all men, and of course the driver and
conductor, and they must have set off that Thursday morning, July 12, in
high old spirits. Naturally there had been previous excursions but this was the
first time the St Mary Cray and Orpington Fire Brigade had hired a bus. Their
previous outings, we must assume, were by train or by Thames steamer or
even by horse-drawn charabanc. This year, however, they would go to
Brighton on a Vanguard bus, an open-topped double-decker, hired from The
London Omnibus Company which, in the previous year, had introduced the
first London to Brighton bus service. Setting off from St Mary Cray at about
eight o'clock on a gloriously bright morning, they picked up members of the
party along the way. All being well, they expected to reach Brighton by one
o'clock or so. What a day, a few chaps out on the spree, away from home, a
day for letting their hair down.

There is no photograph of this 1906 group. We are left to imagine how on
this warm and sunny morning they might have appeared. They ranged from
young boys to men in their fifties. Not all were volunteer firemen: some were
simply friends of brigade members. Many of them appear to have been small
tradesmen: there were at least two bakers, a couple of grocers, a schoolmaster,
a draper, a keeper of a beershop, a clothier and a man who combined the profession of librarian with the trade of basket-maker.

One visualises them as the kinds of men that Wells might write about, men
like Kipps, like Mr Polly, decent sorts, sound friends, cheerful, respectable but
not too prim. We can fancy the older ones among them sporting the substantial
beards of late Victorian days and the younger men with trim Edwardian mous-
taches and sideburns. And on that glowing summer day did some of them
board the bus in stiff serge suits and did others, the more fashionable, rig
themselves out in striped blazers? Were there bowlers and boaters perched
jauntily on pomaded heads?

We know that they sang songs as they bowled along. Witnesses remembered
that, remembered the jolly crew, especially the twenty or so on the open top
deck, and remembered how they waved and called out to them so cheerfully as

68

they sped past at speeds of no less than fifteen miles an hour. They remembered, too, some of them, that the bus was going rather fast, especially with all those chaps standing upstairs.

Some of the party had a beer on the way although there is no suggestion of their having taken any on board. They might have done so. Other parties on similar jaunts took one or more two-gallon barrels with them. Or perhaps this group stopped at a public house. Certainly the driver, Henry Blake, had a couple of drinks, according to one witness, but drink seems to have had no significant part in what was to occur. At least one member of the excursion was a teetotaller and it is not unlikely that there were other total abstainers like him. Such men would have been unwilling to go on a trip of any kind if there had been the slightest hint of immoderate drinking. Laughter, leg-pulling, a few songs and all-round good humour – that would be the order of the day for these kinds of fellows.

The question of speed was later to be a matter of prime concern. But it is extremely difficult to be accurate about this. One estimate of the speed of the Vanguard through Handcross was eight miles an hour. Another put it higher. Three witnesses considered that it had passed through Redhill at too great a speed. There were assertions, too, that the bus had swayed from side to side in its progress through the town. Some attributed this to its speed, others to its having too many passengers on the top deck.

Of course, such road speeds at this time – ignore the speeds of trains – were considered to be quite remarkable if not downright dangerous. But all such assessments of speed from the various observers were guesses, made by people with limited experience of motoring. And even Blake, the driver of bus A3158, could do no more than hazard a guess for the Vanguard had no speedometer.

It was at about eleven o'clock that the bus went through Handcross village and came to the top of a hill which was known to require careful negotiation. It was steep, with a difficult bend, but there should have been no serious difficulty for an experienced driver like Blake, who had driven up and down the hill on several previous occasions and as recently as the Sunday before.

The accident which was about to happen was, according to the *Sussex Daily News*, 'the most dreadful catastrophe which has occurred in the county of Sussex for some time'. Indeed, 'it was the most dreadful disaster which has occurred in this country to a motor bus since this means of locomotion was brought into everyday practical use'.

What happened?

A cyclist walking up the hill on the left side of the road suddenly saw the Vanguard lurching towards him at a terrifying rate. The men on the top of the bus were shouting out, most evidently afraid for their lives. The cyclist was fortunate not to be run down as the vehicle passed closely by him.

In the brickyard on the east side of the road, James Brewer heard a loud clattering and crashing. Looking up, he saw the bus lurch and sway past the entrance. He estimated the speed at fifteen miles per hour. He, too, saw the alarmed passengers on the open upper deck. He also heard the metal parts clanging along the road as they fell off the under parts of the bus.

Yet another cyclist, this one at the top of the hill, was later to say that the bus picked up speed as it began its descent. As it outpaced him, in a swirling cloud of dust from the surface of the poorly maintained road, he heard the shrieks of the frightened men; then, there were two loud bangs and shortly afterwards, he rode over the discarded metal pieces. When he rounded the bend what he saw was to be likened to a railway disaster.

The bus had in its final 100 yards reached perhaps forty miles an hour. On it had gone, spitting so many sparks from underneath that it might have been thought to be on fire. Upstairs, some passengers had clung to the backs of the seats, hoping to save themselves from being catapulted out. Two of them had thrown themselves face down in the gangway as the bus lurched first into one gutter and then wildly across the road, completely out of control despite the driver's attempts to steer it out of danger. Several had attempted to clamber downstairs which added further to the rocking motion of the vehicle. Two others, one a young boy, hurled themselves out of the bus.

Then came the crash. The bus hit an oak tree broadside on. It was almost as if the top deck had been scythed off. With the impact, some of the upstairs passengers were hurled out into the road or against the huge trunk of the oak. Others were jerked high into the air and flung into other roadside trees. Downstairs, bodies were ejected like children's playthings through the plate glass windows. It was as though the Vanguard had burst and scattered its contents 'like the fragments of a gigantic grinding wheel', according to one newspaper report. Machinery, glass, spars of wood, metal seats, personal belongings, were scattered randomly along the road, over the hedges, into the wood beyond.

On the blood-spattered highway lay dead and severely injured; in the ragged growth of hedge was sprawled a corpse; two bodies hung in the trees, one of them suspended upside down. And a boy, in shock, one of those who had jumped from the bus, wandered among other equally dazed victims, calling out for his father. 'Where's my daddy?' he cried. But his undertaker-father lay dead in the woodland beyond, his features quite beyond recognition.

It is remarkable how swiftly people came to the assistance of the stricken men. After all, as locals said, Handcross was 'four miles from everywhere'.

But cyclists and motorists – yes, it was a Thursday and yes again, it was 1906 – raised the alarm and within half an hour doctors and nurses from Crawley, Cowfold, Balcombe and Cuckfield, had arrived in cars and pony-traps and on cycles to do what they could. But for some of those they came to tend, it was already too late. Four had died instantly. Two others, both with broken backs, died shortly afterwards. The rector of nearby Slaugham, the Reverend Mr Boyd, was to relate how, on his arrival, he found the bus in the hedge, up against an oak tree. 'One man who was dying called to me,' he said. 'Another man had his legs torn away and was pinned against the tree by the bus. A leg was left hanging in the tree, clean cut as if with a knife.'

The bodies of the six dead were taken to the Red Lion at Handcross and laid out on straw in a summer-house at the back of the building. Inside the pub, the Club Room was converted into an operating theatre and hospital for the injured. Two of these died later in the day and another of the injured remained on the danger list. Six of the injured were taken to the Cottage Hospital at Crawley and two to the Royal County Hospital in Brighton.

Remarkably, the driver, Henry Blake, had suffered only minor bruising. He had gamely held onto the steering column, wrestling with it until almost the moment of impact, but he had been thrown out just in time to escape the full force of the smash into the oak tree. He was well enough to assist the rescuers in their task and he, along with fourteen others, was judged fit to be sent home by train the same night.

The inquest opened on Saturday, July 14, before the East Sussex Coroner, Mr Vere Benson. The Club Room at the Red Lion underwent yet another conversion and now, small as it was and in unpleasant heat, it accommodated a jury of fifteen, several witnesses and a group of newspaper men representing both the local and national press. On the other inquest days – July 25, August 2, August 7 – the proceedings took place in a large marquee on the lawn at the Red Lion. It was undeniably less disagreeable.

The purpose of the first session of the inquest was to identify the dead, all of whom came from St Mary Cray, with the exception of the recently married Henry Burch, a twenty-six-year-old from Orpington. The others were:

Thomas Francis, forty-nine, baker, father of seven
Henry Hutchings, forty-two, undertaker and volunteer fireman, father of four
William Vann, forty-one, draper, father of two
Edward Packman, thirty-eight, basket-maker and librarian, volunteer fireman, father of two
Solomon Epsom, forty-eight, grocer, widower, father of two
John French, thirty-two, beerhouse keeper, father of two

A gruesome subject for a postcard of the time.

Herbert Baker, forty-three, clothier

Arthur Savage, forty-two, baker, father of eight

The Chelsfield schoolmaster, fifty-four-year-old William Bailey, lingered on in the Club House, until he died, during the following day's inquest.

The accident at Handcross attracted considerable attention, nationally as well as locally. In these early days of motoring, when the vast majority of men and women had never ridden in a petrol-driven engine, it was bound to horrify and to fascinate. There were picture postcards of the Vanguard bus, the hedge and the oak tree almost immediately available; there were also pictures of the bus where it stood in the Red Lion yard covered in tarpaulin. The *Sussex Daily News* described how 'along the road in front of the picturesque old tavern were motor cars, cycles and other vehicles, and it seemed as though an endless procession of motorists and cyclists poured through Handcross all the afternoon'. Among the vast crowds were those who on the Saturday afternoon peered through the hedge towards the summerhouse where the undertakers were lifting the bodies into the coffins.

The jurymen, at the outset, showed some unease about the bus having been moved so quickly from the site of the accident. Was the London Omnibus Company concealing some mechanical defect which had some bearing on what had happened? They were slow to convince that the move had been in the interests of road safety, that to leave the Vanguard where it had come to rest constituted a danger to other road users.

The company came under further hostile fire with the appearance of a witness, Thomas Jones, formerly employed by them as a driver. He came out with some quite alarming statements. The Vanguard, he claimed, was inadequate for Handcross Hill. When he had driven these buses, he had used neither brakes nor gearbox when motoring down the hill; he had always freewheeled down, he said. (The coroner was later to comment very forcefully upon this remarkable practice). Jones stated that if he went down with his brakes on, they were likely to catch fire; if he went down in gear, 'something was likely to go in the gearbox'. The directors of the company, Jones told the court, knew the bus was unsatisfactory. Furthermore, they encouraged him to break the law. They expected him to travel the fifty-two miles to Brighton in four hours. How could it be done without exceeding the speed limit? And then, when he had been fined for speeding only the year before, he had not been reprimanded. In fact, the company had paid his fine.

There were further damaging charges of neglect directed at the company by Jones. On one occasion, he had been unable to use the Vanguard's pinion brake on the poorly maintained roads; another time, the pinion brake was broken and had had to be tied up with wire; then there had been the clutch brake, taken up to the last thread.

All of this was damaging to the company's reputation. Yet Jones was no malcontent; he had not set out to be malicious; he had not even volunteered to give evidence. Having received information from the Local Government Board, the coroner had summoned him to court.

The outing's organiser, Thomas Hoare, a cycle and motor engineer, had sat near the driver during the journey. He was of the view that the bus had functioned badly; the clutch had slipped from the start. Further, Blake had driven too fast through Redhill. Then, when the bus had accelerated on the hill at Handcross, he had expected Blake to apply the brake at once. He had been on the point of tapping the driver's window when he saw him reach for the brake. Then he heard a snapping sound and had seen a large cog in the roadway behind. Then the lurching had begun and it was all too late.

Another witness, admittedly a teetotaller, told the court that he thought that the glasses of beer Blake had taken near Purley and near Gatwick had affected his driving. Others claimed that at Redhill the bus had mounted the pavement and that with several passengers standing upstairs, it had looked top heavy.

For Blake, it has to be said that he was very experienced on both London and country roads. He had passed the test which all bus drivers had to take and he was highly regarded by his employers. Blake explained in court that he was satisfied the bus was running well and that, although he admitted to the clutch slipping early in the journey, he had adjusted this. The brakes were working well and at the top of Handcross Hill he had put on the pinion brake. He was going downhill in third gear and when the bus had unaccountably put on speed he had applied the foot brake but this had had no effect. There had been a deafening bang and the bus had lurched forward. With the foot brake useless and the hand brake immovable, Blake had tried to steer but the bus was completely out of control. He could do nothing to prevent the crash.

As for the bus, experts in court presented its case. The chassis had been built in Germany by Daimler; the body was made in Preston. The bus had travelled 18,000 miles and had had no significant problems, as its record of repairs would show. On the night before the trip, it had been serviced and test-driven. The bus, claimed the experts, was eminently capable of negotiating gradients even steeper than that at Handcross. The Vanguard was a reliable machine; none of its class had previously capsized in this fashion.

When the coroner came to sum up, he asked the jury to consider if there might have been some negligence on the part of the driver. If so, the only verdict was manslaughter. Did the jury think Blake had been driving too fast, thereby endangering his passengers?

Or was the London Omnibus Company at fault? The jury should remember, the coroner advised them, that it was a requirement of the Local Government Board that 'the motor car and fittings shall be in such a condition as not to cause any danger to any person in the motor car or on the highway'. Had the company observed this requirement? Was there, as had been suggested, some hidden weakness in the gear box casing? The coroner stressed that when they came to deliberate, the jury must bear in mind Jones's testimony with all of its implications for the company.

The jurymen retired before nine o'clock to the Club Room which in recent weeks had proved itself to be so versatile. At ten o'clock, in accordance with the strictly observed licensing laws, they were obliged to quit the premises and adjourn to the nearby Mission Room, where they arrived at their verdict at about eleven o'clock.

The jury announced that the fatalities resulted from Vanguard bus, A3158, coming into violent collision with an oak tree. The accident had been caused by the breakage of machinery 'brought on by the efforts of the driver to check the speed of the motor omnibus when he found it was beginning to go too fast, the machinery not being of sufficient strength to stand up to the strain'. The foreman added: 'We consider the driver, Blake, committed an error of judgment in allowing the bus to attain so high a speed before taking means to check it. We do not hold anyone criminally responsible. We are strongly of the opinion that this type of vehicle is unsuitable for use on country roads.'

Blake not guilty? Difficult to say at this distance in time. Perhaps it was the machinery but if so, did the London Bus Company have no responsibility in the matter? Could the accident have been the fault of the passengers upstairs? Had they caused the bus to sway out of control? Or perhaps it was the poor road surface. It had been argued at the inquest that roads such as that where the accident had taken place were 'extremely unsafe for the traffic of today'. Perhaps that was where the cause of the accident lay ... perhaps, perhaps ... a day out ... laughter, leg-pulling, a few songs and all-round good humour – that was what they had all expected ...

SOMETHING DEAD-AHEAD

POLEGATE AIRSHIP CRASH, DECEMBER 22, 1917

WELL before dawn on that raw December day, the ratings were already at work in the corrugated iron sheds, making the pre-flight checks and gassing-up the airships in readiness for take-off. The fact that Christmas was only three days off allowed for no slackening of the war effort.

In contrast, down the road at Eastbourne, three or four miles away, some attempt at normality was being made. There were two pantos, *Robinson Crusoe* and *Pantoland in the Pie*. A vaudeville show called *Champagne* at the Park Pavilion and at Bobby's, *Tea, Toast and Tittle-Tattle*, were advertised in The *Gazette*. Oh and yes, a prominent tradesman in the town had died. There was, of course, some acknowledgement that the war continued with photographs of local men dead in Flanders, missing in Mesopotamia, wounded in Italy. But there was clearly a determined effort to put the war in the background, at least for the time being. It suggests such a pronounced contrast with the purposeful activity at Polegate Naval Air Station where so many of the 300 stationed there were, so early in the day, making ready the five Zero airships for their day's work. The war, its outcome against the Kaiser's Germany still in doubt in 1917, never let up whatever the day.

The airship crews were briefed by the Senior Flying Officer and the Met Officer who had already received reports of good visibility and light winds from the weather stations at Beachy Head and other units along the coast. The airmen ought to have no difficulties in carrying out their tasks of keeping the Channel safe from U-Boats and harassing and destroying any which they sighted. The German submarine menace threatened food supplies and essential materials. The outcome of the war did to some degree depend upon the U-boats being kept in check.

It would be a hard day, that December 22; every man knew that. The crews would fly for at least seven hours – and indeed, on occasion, they had flown spells of up to sixteen hours – and all the time they would be exposed to the biting cold of the upper air and the usual dangers of their work. But there was a proud camaraderie among flyers and ground staff. Morale throughout the service was exceptionally high and so it was at Polegate. Many of the men

A Zero airship flies over the Polegate station in 1917.

stationed there had built the runways, the parade ground, the dining hall, the huge sheds, the men's huts clustered round the windmill, the flower beds. They frequently held concerts and smokers; earlier in the summer of 1917 3,000 people from the surrounding area had attended their sports day. The great fellowship upon which their high morale was based carried them through the difficult days of war. It was to be tested on this day.

Once briefed the crews, each of three men, went to where their airships were tethered outside the shed. Each of the Zeros, its balloon filled with hydrogen, floated just off the ground, restrained by guy-ropes. The men climbed into the eighteen-foot gondola, their three seats one behind the other. It was cramped, certainly, but the Zeros were generally held to be more comfortable than their predecessors despite the fact that the cockpits were not covered.

In front sat the wireless telegrapher/observer. Mounted on a swivel before him was a Lewis gun. Inside his cockpit he carried a Verey pistol; should he need to signal to ships or ground stations he had a daytime signal flap whilst for night he carried an Aldis lamp.

The pilot occupied the centre cockpit, operating the engine controls as well as the supply of gas to the 140ft balloon above.

The mechanic sat at the rear, his main task to ensure the smooth running of the 75hp Rolls Royce engine mounted behind him. Although the Zeros were considered to be very reliable, engine faults did sometimes occur. There were occasions when to locate a fault or to restart a stalled engine, the mechanic was obliged to clamber out of the gondola and swing himself underneath so that he could reach the four-bladed propeller, all the while gripping a strut of the landing carriage between his knees.

How vulnerable they seem, these men in their frail-looking craft with their sixty-gallon cans of petrol, their gas balloon, their two sixty-five pound bombs strapped to the gondola's side. Travelling at a speed of rarely more than sixty miles an hour, they could present easy targets when operating over enemy artillery. When over the sea they were less likely to be brought down by gunfire. In fact the principal concern was that as they carried out so many hours of patrols, their engines might not stand up to such rigorous use. But all in all, the Zeros were immensely popular, 'delightful little ships to handle' according to one enthusiast.

So then, in the early hours of this chill December morning, there was no reason why the five Zeros – Z6, Z7, Z9, Z10 and Z19 – should not leave Polegate with their customary confidence. There were no adverse weather reports, an important consideration for men sitting in their cockpits exposed to the elements.

It was an uneventful morning. No enemy activity was spotted in the Channel; some allied shipping was observed and shadowed but nothing out of the ordinary occurred. Some time in the afternoon came the first indications of a change in the weather. Low cloud had begun to drift in from the north-east. Over a couple of hours, heavier cloud built up, bringing with it drizzle, snow flurries and stronger winds. At three o'clock, with conditions worsening, a decision was taken to recall the airships. With deteriorating visibility, there was no purpose in their continuing to fly.

The airships succeeded in finding their way back to Polegate but cloud and snow had thickened to such a degree that landing there was considered to be dangerous. The congregating craft might crash into each other in the adverse conditions. The ground controllers ordered them to scatter independently and to seek safe landing sites. The next day ground crews would need to be sent out to each location to get the Zeros airborne once more.

Lieutenant John Havers in Z6 flew northwards, landing near Uckfield. After securing the airship, he and his two companions were invited into a grand country house where their dinner was served by the butler. They spent the night there in superb comfort.

Two other airships, Z7 and Z19, turned seawards and found a landing site near the coastguard hut on Beachy Head.

Z10, piloted by Lieutenant Scott, landed in a field at Halfway Farm between

Jevington and Willingdon. The farmer and his twelve-year-old son brought out hot drinks and food. At this spot visibility must have been rather better than in the surrounding area for shortly afterwards Lieutenant Sinclair was able to bring down Z9 only fifty yards or so away from Scott's airship.

There being no telephone at the farm, a member of one of the two crews trudged through the snowy fields to The Eight Bells at Jevington from where Polegate was contacted. It was confirmed that they should stay where they were until the next morning. A ground party from Polegate arrived later to help them with the difficult task of mooring the Zeros in the high wind.

In the next hour or so, the wind from the east strengthened yet more and gale force winds were threatened for later. The Zeros at Jevington were in no danger; they were well enough sheltered in the valley but there was increasing anxiety for the two ships on Beachy Head. The coastguard station was contacted by Polegate and given instructions to pass on to the crews of Z7 and Z19 who were to take advantage of sudden improved visibility and return to their base at once.

The crews, struggling in the fierce wind, readied their craft and climbed into their cockpits, unaided by the usual ground staff assistance. It seems likely that they were helped by the coastguard.

Battling against wind, snow and darkness, Z19 completed the return flight successfully and landed at Polegate.

Z7 took off, flying north across the flat farmland crossing East Dean village and following the valley through the Downs towards Polegate. Her captain, Sub Lieutenant Swallow, had been in the Navy since 1909 and had flown airships

The Z19 comes in to land at Polegate.

79

since 1913. He was very experienced as were both crew members, Victor Dodd the observer and Hughes the mechanic.

Leaning out of the forward cockpit, Dodd, holding the Aldis lamp, picked out the route which in the snow and darkness was barely distinguishable. Flying low, because of the difficulties of visibility, they passed by churches, farm buildings, stables, barns; they crossed fields where sheep huddled in corners; they flew over hedgerows and sometimes alongside frantic shadows of trees, the Aldis light picking up random impressions as they made for Polegate.

But it was too late when Dodd suddenly called out 'Something dead-ahead'.

Lights? Were they at Polegate? A Zero? They could make out the hazy outline of an airship. They could not be sure – was it flying or was it on the ground? But there was no time to manoeuvre. It was too late when Swallow tried to climb out of danger. The bottom of his gondola tore the top of Z10's balloon. At once, they could hear the hiss of escaping hydrogen.

Too late for Z7. The escaping gas was straightaway ignited by her exhaust.

'All for yourselves, lads,' Swallow shouted as a sheet of fire engulfed his craft. The two crewmen, Dodd and Hughes, struggled out of their confined cockpits and jumped into the fields below. The airship, its load lighter now, rose 2,000-3,000ft through the falling snow, up into the darkened sky. And then, like some dying comet, it fell towards the ground.

Flames from its own balloon had engulfed the stationary Z10 by now. Her crew were still in their cockpits, scarcely having had time to realise the situation they were in. The crew of Z9, however, had seen all that had occurred since first they had been aware of the beam of Dodd's Aldis lamp heralding the approach of Z7. Seeing their comrades were in danger, they ran across to the burning airship. They pulled the men to safety. In the confusion Lieutenant Victor Watson, who was in charge of the ground party, mistakenly believed that one of the crew was still aboard and returned to the craft. Just as he arrived, the airship's two sixty-five pound bombs exploded, injuring him severely and tearing off an arm.

Simultaneously, other members of the ground party, air mechanic Harold Robinson and boy mechanic Eric Steere, had dashed as fast as they were able across the snowy field to where the wreckage of Z7 still burned. They found the pilot dead in the cockpit. Sub Lieutenant Swallow is buried in Ocklynge Cemetery.

With incredible courage, Robinson and Steere, ignoring the fierce heat, snatched the bombs from the airship and carried them away. Their hands were cruelly blistered but they had saved another explosion.

Later in the evening, Dodd and Hughes, who had been seriously injured in

Tragedy on Jevington Down where the Z7 crashed in flames.

their jump from the Zero, were given medical attention at the farm and were then taken to Eastbourne Hospital, along with Lieutenant Watson.

A Court of Enquiry held shortly afterwards at Newhaven attached no blame to any individual. This was, according to the verdict, an instance of 'sheer bad luck combined with appallingly difficult weather conditions'.

'For distinguished acts of bravery', Watson, Robinson and Steere were awarded the Albert Medal.

Only days after the disaster, the first edition of the station's magazine was published. *The Ripping Panel* is cheerful, witty, dignified. It contains poems, ironic comments, satirical articles, humorous prose. It makes no mention of the fate of Swallow, the loss of two Zeros, the wonderful courage which their comrades displayed. The Royal Naval Airship Station at Polegate simply got on with its task, continuing its gallant work modestly and efficiently for the rest of the war.

IN THE TWINKLING OF AN EYE

THE LOSS OF THE RYE LIFEBOAT, NOVEMBER 15, 1928

NOT twenty minutes ago the maroon was fired, briefly lighting up the sky and rousing most of those who slept. Out of beds, out of houses, into the road they stumble. It is as black as blindness at this early hour and some of them carry hurricane lamps, though these cast only a narrow circle of light on the ground. For the past twenty-four hours weather conditions have been vile, among the worst in living memory. The shrieking wind rages with such ferocity that these people, forty, fifty of them, have to lean into it so that its force does not bowl them over. Icy needles of rain, tingling sand, sea spray which will find its way four miles inland, cut down visibility to a few yards. But of this discomfort the men and women take little heed. All thoughts are on the sea, a mile down the road from the village. The sea can be heard from far off as it boils, thunders, crashes, hurtles on the beach. So here then is the crew of the lifeboat, *Mary Stanford*, men from tiny Rye Harbour, stepping out this dark and angry November morning in their oilskins, their seaboots, their life jackets, towards the unforgiving sea. And with them come the launchers who will do their muscle-bursting task, will wrestle, drag, heave till they have the boat and its crew in the waters. There are all sorts of engines available in this year of 1928, in this sophisticated technological age. Yet at Rye Harbour on this wretched day it is muscle-power that has to be relied upon.

There are others, too, accompanying crew and launchers. There are wives and mothers; brothers, uncles. They are come to see off the *Mary Stanford* in an eighty mile an hour south-westerly. They know that all along the channel boats have sought refuge. They know, too, that the *Alice*, a Latvian ship, has lost her rudder and is drifting helplessly eight miles off Dungeness. What they do not know is that a German ship, the *Smyrna*, is already poised to take off the crew from the stricken ship.

It is low tide, the towering waves half a mile out across the beach, and the lifeboat, four and a half tons in weight, has to be hauled across the sand. The crew and the launchers, now on each side of the 38ft long craft, urge it with back-breaking effort towards the sea.

Although they left their cottages shortly after five this November morning, the launchers do not have the *Mary Stanford* in the sea much before six forty-five. They have struggled deep in the water up to their chests while the waves constantly pound down on them with an unremitting force. Twice they have had the boat out to sea, and twice the sea has thrown her back and in doing so has threatened their lives. Only on the third try is the launch successful. Now the men on shore are exhausted. They watch the crew bending their backs to the oars, no motor engine on this vessel, until in a brief minute she disappears into the dark.

The crew, out in the great waters, are heroes already. They are seventeen in number; the oldest of them, Bert Head, forty-seven-year-old cox, is a father of five. The youngest in the boat are his two sons, nineteen-year-old James and seventeen-year-old John. Others heaving against the sea this morning are the Cutting brothers, Robert (twenty-eight) and Henry (thirty-nine); the Downey cousins, Morris (twenty-three) and Arthur (twenty-five); the Clark brothers, Leslie (twenty-four) and William (twenty-seven); the Pope brothers, Charles, Robert and Alex (twenty-eight, twenty-three and twenty-one). With them is the second cox, another father of five, forty-three-year-old Joseph Stonham. Albert Smith (forty-four), Walter Igglesden (thirty-eight) and Charles Southerden (twenty-two) make up the crew. They are all fishermen, all experienced seamen.

Had these men had time to look up from their work at the oars they would have seen nothing in that impenetrable morning light. But they had no chance to gaze about them; they were fighting the sea. Nor did they know that within five minutes of their departure Verey lights and men calling through loud hailers tried to get them back, for a message had come in to the Lifeboat Station. The *Smyrna* had taken the crew of the *Alice* on board. The abandoned ship had been left to fend for herself, and she would be finally submerged later that day.

In the roaring storm the calls to return were not heard, the flares not seen. The *Mary Stanford* went out further to do her duty, to continue her now pointless mission. Unseen for more than two hours, she battled against the awesome waves. At times the sail was up; at other times the men used the oars. Their work now called for seamanship of the highest order, but then Bert Head was held to be 'the most skilful seaman in a port famed for hardy mariners'.

At 9am the lifeboat was spotted three miles WSW off Dungeness by the mate of the SS *Halton*. He was to report that, despite very high seas and frequent rain squalls, the *Mary Stanford* seemed to be going well enough. She had two small lug sails set.

There was no other sighting of her until about 10.30am when she was in Rye Bay, fighting her way back home. It seems that Head, aware that it was too late to do any good, called off the rescue and had intended to put in to

The self-righting Mary Stanford, dependent upon sail and oars. Picture: RNLI.

Folkestone. Finding the seas too violent, however, he had decided to run for Rye. A young boy, Charles Marchant, collecting driftwood on the beach, spotted the *Mary Stanford* in the improving light. 'I saw the boat going along towards the harbour about two miles out to sea. Then suddenly it seemed as if there was a gust of wind and I saw her turn right over and disappear,' he said.

Another witness said that the lifeboat went from sight 'in the twinkling of an eye'. Others also saw this dreadful mishap. All of them rushed to raise the alarm.

There was no warning for the observers, no indication of any momentous struggle. The *Mary Stanford* was battling through the water as she must have done since first she set off and then, in seconds, she had capsized and was lost to view.

There were already people waiting on the beach. This was the shore party, called out earlier by maroon to help the lifeboat ashore. Now they were joined on that inhospitable stretch of sand by doctors, coastguards, police. Yet others set off down the coast in the direction of Dungeness in the hope that they might even now be of some help to the stricken lifeboatmen. Members of the crew's families came to the shore also, waiting under heavy grey skies, in the fierce gusting winds, in the frequent torrential downpours.

At some time late in the morning the *Mary Stanford* was hurled on to the beach by the crashing waves, lying there upturned and refusing stubbornly to be righted until a tank, brought from Lydd, was able to turn her over. Only then were two bodies found, wedged in the seats.

As the afternoon wore on more bodies were washed up until finally fifteen were accounted for. Artificial respiration was tried in every case but with no success. One corpse was to turn up on Eastbourne beach months later. Another was never recovered.

The *Hastings Observer* wrote of the extent of this tragedy, the worst British lifeboat disaster since 1886: 'There is hardly a house in the little fishing village by the Rother mouth that has not lost a husband, a father or son.'

Certainly, blood links were strong and reinforced by marriages in this close-knit community. Few living there were untouched by the events of that morning. Yet, there was a stoicism about the people waiting on the bleak beach. 'Bred in the tradition of the sea,' the *Observer* commented, 'these simple people bore their great sorrow calmly. For generations the sea has given them life and too often the sea has taken it away. But rarely has it dealt them a more cruel blow.'

At five o'clock that evening the inquest on six of those recovered on Camber Sands was opened in the Mission Hall and it was as though the elements were contriving to remind those inside why they were there. The wind rattled windows and doors and regularly searched under the roof so that it rose and fell with echoing crashes throughout the proceedings. So loud was the wind that the witnesses had to shout to be heard. The paraffin lamps flickered and flared while the sand continuously spattered against the window panes.

The inquest held over two days raised a number of searching questions. Had this been a needless waste of life? Was the communication system good enough? What was the condition of the equipment? Was this lifeboat safe? The questions were searching but ultimately no coroner's court was adequate to answer them.

Police Sergeant Anthony was challenged about artificial respiration by Captain Strange, Inspector of HM Coastguard (Hove). For how long had artificial respiration been given, the policeman was asked. When he replied up to three hours, the coastguard captain responded:

'Do you know our men are instructed to go on for five or six hours?'

'No.'

'Well, they are.'

'There were no signs of life in any of them,' Sergeant Anthony answered. 'Those in the water were continually battering against the breakwater. No man could live in a sea like that.'

One crew member had not answered the call that morning. Living out at Udimore, Major Hacking had not heard the warning maroon. He told the coroner that the men's life jackets had perished and that they would have been quickly waterlogged. They would be no use to their wearers. This was disturbing and clearly further investigation was required.

There were also questions about the crucial message received at Rye Lifeboat House. Had there been some delay, either at Rye Harbour or earlier at Ramsgate Coastguard Station whence the message had been passed to the Rye Coastguard? Captain Strange was concerned that the coroner was not following up these matters strenuously enough.

'Then you are not calling any more technical evidence,' he said. 'My concern is the SOS. We are responsible for the lifeboat being informed. I was trying to find out if there had been any delay with our messages, but apparently there had not.'

The coroner replied: 'The question has not arisen.' But the question had most certainly arisen. A verdict of accidental death was reached but the underlying queries remained to be resolved. As a consequence, the Board of Trade appointed a Commission of Enquiry to look into the whole matter of the Rye Lifeboat disaster.

The Commission was convened at Rye Town Hall on December 19. Between then and January 4, 1929 it met and took evidence on seven days.

The Commission considered the suitability of the *Mary Stanford* for her task. This Liverpool-type boat was not self-righting but it had other virtues. In 1914 members of the crew had visited Cromer where this model was in service. On the strength of what they had seen they proposed to bring it to Rye Harbour and the crew voted for it. One major advantage was that it was less cumbersome than its predecessor, a self-righting model. Rye was a notoriously difficult beach on which to launch a lifeboat and for this reason the *Mary Stanford* was chosen. Even she was not easy to get to sea: how much worse the other boats must have been.

Since coming to Rye in 1916, there had been forty-seven practice rescues and the boat had been out on active service on fifteen occasions. In all 127 people had been saved by the *Mary Stanford*. The crew liked her and the Commission was to declare its opinion that she was 'quite suitable'.

As to the life jackets, described by one witness as 'drowning jackets', this type had been used by the Rye crew since 1917. Although other crews had complained of their being uncomfortable and inconvenient, the Rye crew had voted to use them and continued to express their satisfaction with them. Whether they were perished, as Hacking said, seems not to have been explored. The Commission judged itself not competent to say what had happened to the life jackets or how they functioned once the crew went into the water. 'Neither is it possible to say,' the report states, 'that the life jackets caused or contributed to the loss of life.'

The major issue related to the communication of messages on the day of the disaster. The Commission heard that North Foreland Radio Station had originated a message which was sent at 4.27am to Ramsgate Coastguard. At 4.50am Rye Coastguard received the message: 'Steamer Alice, Riga – leaking – danger – drifting SW to W, eight miles from Dungeness, 0430.'

The time lags here are possibly of no consequence. This was an especially busy watch, ships all along the Channel being in greater or lesser danger. It is likely that many urgent messages were being dealt with simultaneously. The maroons which roused the sleeping village and which set the men and women of Rye Harbour on the road to the beach went off at about 5am. It was to take until 6.45am for the *Mary Stanford* to put out to sea.

What really was to concern the Commission was what happened to the message which said that the crew had been taken off the *Alice* and were now safely aboard the *Smyrna*. Why had that information not been more speedily conveyed to the Rye crew? When they set out, it had been known at Ramsgate for over half an hour that the Latvian crew was safe. Had there been undue delay in transmitting the message? The Commission also considered a second question – what measures had been taken at Rye to recall the boat once it was launched?

It transpired that the Rye men were victims of procedural arrangements which did not accord priority to a telephone message not relaying emergency

The Mary Stanford, hurled on to the beach, contained the bodies of two of the crew, wedged in the seats. Picture: RNLI.

information. Now that the *Alice* was safe, there was no longer any emergency. On that violent morning, other matters, current emergencies, were at the top of the list. The *Alice* sank in importance: the *Mary Stanford* sank.

The Commission recommended that in future 'any messages which may affect the lifeboat should be given priority as life-saving messages'.

Referring to the attempts to recall the lifeboat at Rye, the Commission acknowledged that flares had been fired and loud hailers used, but that in such desperate weather these had been ineffective. They made the observation that the recall flag had not been hoisted as it ought to have been, though it was acknowledged that it would not have been seen.

As to the cause of the capsize, that was a matter of conjecture. 'In the absence of any direct evidence the Commission came to the conclusion that the capsizing of the lifeboat was probably due to the fact that, in attempting to make the harbour in a strong flood tide and in heavy, dangerous and breaking seas, with a gale of wind in her quarters, she capsized and the crew were thrown into the water and drowned.'

The Rye lifeboat disaster touched the hearts of the nation. A relief fund raised £35,000 for dependents in the space of weeks. There were memorial services in churches and chapels throughout the land. The funeral attracted a procession of mourners two miles long.

The *Hastings Observer* summed up the feeling of the time. 'The tragedy was tempered by the proud knowledge that seventeen men from this tiny cluster of cottages in this lonely corner of England had thrilled the whole country by the heroic manner of their death.'

The memorial in the churchyard at Rye Harbour is surmounted by the statue of a fisherman. It says: 'We have done that which it was our duty to do.'

The memorial to the crew of the Mary Stanford in the churchyard at Rye Harbour.

CITY OF FRIGHTENED PEOPLE?

THE BRIGHTON SMALLPOX OUTBREAK 1950-1951

IT WAS December 27, some time around midday, when the office of Brighton's Medical Officer of Health took a phone call from Bevendean Isolation Hospital. They were concerned about the condition of a couple of patients. One of them, twenty-six-year-old Elsie Bath, a GPO telephonist, had been admitted several days earlier and had, throughout her stay, been very poorly. Now her father had reported to the hospital and had been detained. Harold Bath's symptoms were similar to those of his daughter. Both had thought that they were victims of the influenza outbreak which had in recent days affected many in the town and which was especially virulent that winter in the north and midlands. But the hospital doctors were convinced that these two patients had smallpox.

Smallpox? In England? In 1950? Hadn't it been all but eradicated? There had been terrible outbreaks years ago but it was the disease that older people talked about. Very few people now had any experience of it. Eighty years earlier, in the winter of 1871-1872, there had been 44,000 cases recorded in Britain. But that was all in the past. Admittedly, mass vaccination had waned in popularity in recent years for it killed more children than would have died without it. But the menace of the disease had been conquered in Britain so how could there now be smallpox here? In Brighton of all places?

But the MOH, Doctor Rutherford Cramb, agreed with the diagnosis made by medical staff at Bevendean that the father and daughter had contracted smallpox. For confirmation, specimens were sent to the laboratories at Colindale but no-one had any doubt that this was an emergency of the first magnitude and that delay in taking positive action would lead to the spread of what is probably the most contagious disease known to medical science. It ravages whole communities in certain parts of the world. If it were not immediately controlled, then it might do the same in Brighton. And it would, most assuredly, in that case, spread to other parts of the country. The death toll could be unimaginably high. The smallpox outbreak, identified that day in Brighton, was a threat to the whole of the country. Was this to be a disaster that would destroy thousands of lives?

Cramb's immediate problem was time. How long did he have before the disease spread? Who had Elsie Bath been in contact with prior to her admission to Bevendean? And how many had had dealings with her in hospital? These were all potentially vulnerable. There could be people walking the streets of Brighton and neighbouring Hove who were already infected. And her father, what about him? He was a taxi driver who had worked over the busy Christmas period. He must have had hundreds of fares. And where had Elsie picked up the germ which she had so evidently passed on to her father? Was it possible that some stranger with whom she had been in fleeting contact had infected her? Why, even now, someone might still be out and about unknowingly infecting others.

When Elsie Bath was questioned that afternoon, however, the medical staff realised that she knew the person who had infected her. Her fiancé, a flight lieutenant in the Royal Air Force, she told them, had recently returned from a posting in India and he had stayed with her in Brighton when he was on leave. Not that he had been much fun for from his arrival at her house on November 29 until he had gone to his new posting in Scotland on December 14, he had been constantly ill. Malaria, they had thought.

It was now desperately important to find Flight Lieutenant Hunter. Cramb had no doubt that he was a prime source of the infection. His commanding officer must get hold of the man and have him sent to hospital for a check-up. But Elsie Bath told the doctors questioning her that Hunter was not in Scotland now. He was back in Brighton again. On December 22 he had come down as arranged to spend his Christmas leave but, of course, by then she was in hospital with this dratted flu or bug or whatever it was. Anyway, he seemed all right now. He had recovered from whatever had ailed him and now he was right as rain. His leave was due to end today. As a matter of fact, he was going to call in to see her before he caught the train back up to Scotland.

When, later in the day, Hunter arrived at Bevendean, he was questioned. He had had malaria, he told the doctor, but it had cleared up. Well yes, there had been a bit of a rash. On the forehead and on his wrists, too, but there was no sign of that now. He had been revaccinated a few weeks earlier, Hunter said. In this, he was not telling the truth. Vaccination does cause some discomfort and he had avoided his jab. In fairness, he probably thought that it was completely unnecessary. After all, Hunter had had vaccinations as an infant and in 1943 and just the previous year, 1949.

Elsie Bath and Hunter were sent off at once to Longreach Smallpox Hospital at Dartford. Hunter's Commanding Officer was informed and in consequence several thousand airmen were vaccinated. Some who were on leave were ordered not to return to their stations but to be vaccinated by their local GPs and to stay on leave a further sixteen days by which time they would be beyond the incubation period.

Harold Bath was too ill to travel and he died within hours of his daughter's departure. His taxi was found and disinfected. Because he had belonged to a co-operative of owner-drivers with a centralised booking system, it was possible to trace most of the journeys he had made and most of his passengers. Telegrams of advice were sent to Medical Officers of Health for the areas from which these people came. Thus, out of the blue, Devonians and Scotsmen, Ulstermen and Geordies were approached by their local health departments and advised about what to do.

As soon as confirmation of smallpox was received from Colindale at teatime on the following day, December 28, the health department's plans – and thank goodness, there had been long-standing preparation for such an eventuality, no matter how unlikely it might have seemed only days earlier – were implemented. All staff and patients at Bevendean were vaccinated. All living-out and part-time staff had to be found. They and their families were vaccinated. Not that this meant that everyone was safe. Only forty-two per cent of these people, many of whom had not been vaccinated previously, were treated successfully. That is, not all vaccinations took although, mercifully, they did not all fall victim to the disease. But anyone, vaccinated or not, might still, after ten days or so, display the symptoms, might experience the headaches, the heightened temperature, the aching back and the rashes on the face, on the forehead, on the hands and ankles. All were in danger. Some of those now being vaccinated were already beyond hope though at this point they were ignorant of the fact.

What has been described as the biggest manhunt in Sussex was now set in motion. In the space of two weeks, 5,000 people, not solely in Brighton but scattered throughout the British Isles, were sought and found and it was the Brighton Health Department and in particular the sixteen sanitary inspectors, aided by three others seconded for the work from East Sussex County Council, who bore the burden of the seek and find operation. Every possible contact was sought. Friends, metermen, shop assistants, workmates, members of darts teams and Sunday football players were found. So were members of Women's Institutes and regular attenders at weekly whist drives. Brides and their guests, bridegrooms and their stag-night pals were visited. Over the two weeks this task-force performed remarkably, travelling jointly thousands of miles to examine those they had tracked down for traces of the frightening disease. If they found anything unusual, they called the doctor. Their results were of prime importance for they identified several cases which were likely, had they not been recognised, to have led to a spreading of the outbreak.

Christmas had, not unnaturally, been an especially busy time at Bevendean Hospital. There had been, as expected, a great number of visitors. Religious and charitable organisations had sent in representatives. There had been the usual range of entertainers, carol singers and the like. On Christmas Day, the mayor and other councillors had toured the hospital. In addition, there had been scores of visitors from other parts of the country. All of these had to be found and warned. An urgent broadcast from the BBC appealed for all who had been to Bevendean since Elsie Bath's admission on December 18 to get in touch with their GPs.

There were other pressing matters. The local public health laboratory was requested to build up lymph stock for who knew how many might need to be vaccinated before this frightening disease had run its course. Then, what about other places? Who knows how many people had come to Brighton in recent weeks and had moved on? Brighton was a regional centre, just the ideal place to visit for Christmas shopping, for the panto, for the ice show, for holiday treats. Neighbouring health departments were sent the appropriate information, not so that they would necessarily want to treat the matter as an emergency but so that, in the event of their experiencing a similar outbreak, they would have had time to prepare appropriate procedures.

Elsie Bath's workmates at the GPO Telephone Exchange needed to be informed of the situation. On December 29, the men and women on all shifts were visited by sanitary inspectors who explained that Elsie, who had been away ill for eleven days, had smallpox. They needed to be vaccinated. To add point to the argument, they were able to say that Harold Bath had died that day and that of two other patients with similar symptoms, just admitted to hospital, one was from the exchange. Any operators who had not turned up for work were visited at home, examined and vaccinated.

Over the holiday period, even though his fiancée was in hospital, Flight Lieutenant Hunter had been to public houses and dances and parties. Naturally so. But tracing those random social links was extraordinarily complex. Two of the airman's contacts subsequently contracted the disease. Now, in turn, their contacts had to be sought. With each widening of the circle, so did the danger of a wholesale disaster seem likely.

A hospital admission on December 30 indicated another danger area. A laundry worker was diagnosed as being infected. The following day, another worker was similarly diagnosed. Soiled linen from Elsie Bath's house had gone to the branch collecting office of the local laundry on December 7, 14 and 21. Now, the main laundry was investigated. Some of the sorters of dirty linen had fallen ill. Added to this was the unfortunate complication that these

92

workers, now potentially infectious, had on some days packed newly laundered articles ready for despatch. Thus, customers were now at risk. The laundry was immediately closed down and 1,900 customers sought out and warned.

Although the whole response to the peril was immaculately organised, there were difficulties which had to be overcome. Undertakers, for example, refused to handle the body of the dead taxi-driver and the crematorium would not deal with the coffin. These tasks became the responsibility of health department staff throughout the period of the outbreak.

The main routes of the spread of infection were identified as the laundry which had been closed, the telephone exchange where it was deemed safe to continue working for the time being, and the hospital at Bevendean. The decision was taken on December 29 to close off the hospital to the outside. Like the inhabitants of some medieval village in the plague years, the staff locked themselves inside the walls with those who might well within days infect them. From now no new admissions would be allowed. These would have to be sent up to the smallpox hospital in Dartford. As things turned out on this vilest of winters, with the snow blocking some major roads and the surfaces of others glassy and treacherous with hard packed ice, journeys to Dartford for some days after January 2 proved impossible. From then, it was to Foredown Hospital at Portslade that patients had to be sent. It too was closed to the outside world. Only after a week were admissions to Dartford resumed. Nurses from many neighbouring hospitals – Eastbourne, Brighton County, Canterbury among them – volunteered to work both at Dartford and Portslade, knowing the potential dangers of the task.

For Bevendean and Foredown, special arrangements had to be made with the outside world. Hove General Hospital, for instance, became the supply depot for Foredown. Drugs, medical equipment, ice-cream, newspapers and a whole host of other quite ordinary personal requirements were taken by van and left just outside the hospital gates to be picked up by staff. Dr Lennhoff, a German doctor, worked at both hospitals, travelling between the two each day in her Ford 8. After each journey, her car was disinfected. She did not even fill up with petrol at local garages. Instead, there were special stocks of petrol and oil for her at Bevendean. Had her car broken down in the wretched winter weather, the complications would have been considerable, both for her and for the authorities.

The ambulance service continued to work selflessly although special precautions were essential. Each time smallpox patients were taken to the hospitals, the vehicles were scrupulously disinfected. After each journey, the clothing of the ambulance men was changed and sterilised.

The 'No Admittance' notices go up at Foredown Hospital, Portslade.

As for the beleaguered nursing staff and the patients at the two hospitals, their links with the outside world were principally by letter. The majority of households had no telephone at that time. Patients' letters were written on special cards which were sterilised and then taken to the post box in sterilised bags.

There can be no doubting the heroic devotion to duty of the staffs, both medical and domestic, at Beyendean and Portslade and, of course, at Dartford. They were not to know how many of their number were infected. The first days were without doubt extremely trying for them. Only when the incubation period was over, after sixteen days, would the situation be clear. Out of twenty-nine confirmed and six unconfirmed cases dealt with in the three hospitals between December 29 and February 7, there were ten deaths. Harold Bath, the taxi driver, and a forty-eight-year-old domestic worker died at Bevendean. In all, Dartford received nineteen patients including the six unconfirmed, as well as Elsie Bath and her fiancé, both of whom were cleared. The four dead at Dartford included a twenty-eight-year-old nurse and a student nurse, both from Bevendean; a twenty-year-old grocery assistant, and a gardener from Bevendean Hospital whose only contact with patients was to remove a Christmas tree from a ward.

Fourteen cases were sent to Portslade. There were four deaths, including

94

two nurses and a domestic worker from Bevendean and a laundry worker.

Not until February 2, after thirty-four days, was Dr Cramb able to lift the quarantine imposed upon the hospitals. On that day, Bevendean was able to send the patients, 107 of them, to their homes. Fifty overjoyed nurses and thirty-six general staff were also released and sent off on fourteen days' leave. In their absence the hospital was to be disinfected, washed down, fumigated.

At the time, there is no doubt that the town was seriously affected. Not, of course, to the degree that some of the national Sunday press claimed. Despite what the London headline writers wanted to make of it – 'The City of Frightened People' was one sub-editor's contribution – there was no panic. People went to the clinics or to their GPs for vaccination, often being obliged to queue in snow, ice and rain. Indeed, more than 70,000 were vaccinated in Brighton and Hove. And yet, in retrospect, it all seems very matter of fact. Life and all its multifarious activities went on with some inevitable disruptions. It was certainly not brought to a standstill.

Throughout the period, the *Evening Argus* maintained a constantly level-headed position, reporting what was occurring but at no time was there any shrill quality in its reports. In fact, the outbreak, after the first day or so, was kept off the front page. There were sound reasons for this. If the smallpox scare were given too much prominence, it might increase anxiety. Sensationalism could only worsen matters. And in any case, the population of Brighton and Hove had stood up to other dangers in the recent past. If they had not succumbed to the Brighton Blitz, they were unlikely to find the present problem overwhelming.

There were some flurries. When a young man, who later died, was first committed to hospital, the grocer's shop at which he worked was closed. The stock was destroyed and even the customers' ration books were collected and burned. A ten-year-old boy, whose mother had died of smallpox, was taken to hospital and some parents refused to send their children back to the school at the end of the holidays. The authorities had asked that only those who had not been vaccinated should stay away: the rest they wanted to attend school in order to be able to keep an eye on them. Some sports fixtures were cancelled but it is remarkable how life seems to have gone on without too much disruption. Some people in Crowborough, Worthing, Hailsham and other towns, who had visited shows in Brighton, had an anxious time until the incubation period was over and they found they had nothing to worry about.

Up in Edmonton, a Brighton man, who thought he had found a job on the dustcart, was surprised to find that within half an hour of his appointment, he was dismissed. They were not going to work with a man from Brighton. Then, there was the official at the Air Ministry who refused to handle some programmes relating to ATC activities on the grounds that they were to be printed in Brighton. And there were complaints that at Victoria someone on the platform had called out 'All aboard for the Plague Special'. Bad taste, perhaps, though that is sometimes how men and women face up to the perceived dangers of the world.

All in all, however, both in Brighton and outside the dangers were faced up to with courage and intelligence by the medical profession and what seems like a stoic acceptance on the part of the people of Brighton and Hove.

The Brighton smallpox outbreak, with its most terrifying of possibilities, came and left in the freezing grimness of the post-Christmas period. It came with such a horrifying swiftness, leaving in its wake its customary legacy. Its visit was a disaster but considering what havoc it might have wreaked, it is fair to call it, with some relief and with untold gratitude to those who fought it, a minor disaster.

A GRAND OCCASION

THE SINKING OF THE EASTBOURNE
FLYING BOAT, JUNE 4, 1955

THERE is little a town likes better than a grand occasion, something to put it centre stage, something that encourages it to show itself off to best advantage. And especially when it welcomes many visitors and VIPs and most particularly when a member of the royal family is invited to participate in the proceedings. So when Eastbourne was chosen to host the Silver Jubilee Conference of the Royal Air Force Association in 1955 there was a considerable degree of self-congratulation, the more so as its president, Prince Philip, the Duke of Edinburgh, was to be in attendance.

Out came the bunting; out came the council's paint pots; out came the flower baskets on standards which, surmounted by golden crowns, had not been used since the Coronation. On Saturday June 4, and on the following day the town was to be *en fête*. And, of course, huge crowds were expected just to glimpse the royal visitor who for most was no more than a fuzzy picture on a nine-inch television screen. Even so – and it is a contrast with later times – there was no call for help from adjoining police forces. The local force could cope, with the support of special constables.

The prince was scheduled to arrive at midday on the Saturday. He would alight from his helicopter on the Western Lawns, a gracious open space overlooking the sea at the western end of the town. Here he would be met by the Duke of Norfolk, Lord Tedder, Marshal of the Royal Air Force, and various civic dignitaries. After lunch at the Grand Hotel, he would preside over meetings of the association in the Winter Garden. He would spend the night at the Burlington Hotel. The following day there was to be an open-air service on the Western Lawns and a march-past, after which the Duke would be whisked away to polo at Cowdray Park. It was an occasion which the town anticipated with excitement.

This was the biggest conference the Royal Air Force Association had ever held. Members from 700 local associations were due to arrive in town. RAF Coastal Command had decided to mark the event. On the Saturday the *Eastbourne Herald* announced: 'A flying boat from 19 Group, Coastal

Command, will arrive at about 10 o'clock this morning, land off shore and stay there until 7.0 p.m. Air-sea rescue launches and tenders arrived yesterday and are anchored off the sea front. The flying boat will return at about 9.45 tomorrow morning.'

This twenty-four ton symbol seemed so fitting for such an occasion.

Just as the newspaper had written, the Sunderland flying boat appeared over Eastbourne at 9 o'clock and for the next half hour in the bright summer sky it circled slowly over the town. It then made its descent, landing in a north-south direction a mile or so out to sea, watched by the excited crowds who lined the sea front.

A man watching from the beach was to say: 'It seemed to me a perfect landing'. He watched the plane taxi for a hundred yards or so. Then everything happened so suddenly, so unexpectedly. At one moment the flying boat appeared to be on an even keel on the surface of the water. Then, inexplicably, the tail shot up in the air and the whole aircraft was quickly submerged in a dense spray. Finally, it appeared to settle gently, just below the surface of the water.

Another witness described how, after a short time, he saw figures emerging from the waves, scrambling on to the starboard wing. The RAF launches standing by rushed to the scene. So, too, did the Eastbourne lifeboat, *Beryl Tollemache*, and the pleasure boat *William Allchorn*, skippered by Sam

The smoke float attached to the fuselage ignited and there was a danger of the fuel tanks blowing. Frogmen went out from the beach to help the trapped airmen.

A naval frogman walks on the wing as the Sunderland settles in the water.

Allchorn. A boat manned by fishermen joined the search for survivors.

In all, ten men out of the fourteen on board were taken ashore and thence to hospital. Missing were the pilot, Flight Lieutenant T R Gush; the second navigator, Flying Officer A E Doran; Master Engineer T Body and the only Sussex member of the crew, Leading Aircraftsman J K Rothwell of Peacehaven.

The search for the missing men went on for several hours. Naval frogmen were flown in by helicopter from Portsmouth. It was only after the lifeboat and Allchorn's pleasure boat had put a hawser round the hull of the Sunderland and had towed it near the shore that the four bodies were discovered. Two of the men had drowned; two had died from multiple injuries.

It was at this point, with the aircraft now on the beach, that another serious accident was averted. A smoke float attached to the fuselage ignited and there was danger of the petrol tanks exploding. Fortunately, local firemen succeeded in extinguishing the flames in time. The following Wednesday, there was another narrow escape. Airmen cutting through part of the wing with an acetylene torch caused a petrol tank to explode. Remarkably, only one man of the four involved was injured. He had a broken leg.

Naturally, there were rumours as to what had caused the accident. Some asserted that the flying boat had fouled a cable attached to a buoy marking the wreckage of a motor boat from Dover which had sunk in a gale some time previously. But local fishermen were quick to deny this possibility. They knew these waters.

At the inquest on June 7 it was said that it would take four weeks for an RAF Board of Enquiry to assess the causes of the accident. The coroner commented that 'this very tragic accident taking place in such circumstances on such an occasion must be deplored by all'. Indeed, there was a fierce irony in the event intended to honour the many ex-RAF members visiting the town and those whom they represented.

It is interesting to note, however, that the Sunderland flying boat's tragic accident was restricted to four brief paragraphs in the local newspaper on June 8, whilst six pages contained full descriptions and several photographs of the visit of the Duke of Edinburgh and the conference of the Royal Air Force Association. A telegram was sent to the relatives of the dead men. The *Eastbourne Herald* observed with some approval that the telegram 'had been written and signed by the Duke'. Later in the week, the newspaper made much of the Queen Mother's meeting with the Mayor and Mayoress of Eastbourne at a function at Eridge. She told them how much Prince Philip had enjoyed his week-end in the town. It was of course, despite the dreadful accident, not unreasonable that he should have enjoyed the occasion. It is the fact that the newspaper yet again offers so little information about the accident that, on the face of it, seems totally remiss. Was the editor asked by the RAF to keep his report low key? Tragic though it was, perhaps the RAF did not wish this occasion, significant for so many ex-airmen, to be overshadowed by what could be described as a working accident.

The inquest was resumed in late July. The court was reminded that the aircraft had set off from Calshot with eleven crew and three passengers. Nothing untoward occurred during the flight. The first navigator, Flying Officer Michael Owtram, told the court that they had made a good landing at about eighty-five knots and touched down beside the control launch. 'After that,' he said, 'I had no notion of time but the next thing I remember was being under the water. I swam through the pilot's canopy, inflated my Mae West and climbed on the wing of the aircraft.'

Another crew member, the wireless operator, Sergeant Geoffrey Bevis, was sitting behind the pilot as they came in to land. He had warned the crew that in view of the sea-swell the landing might be rough. As it was, all seemed to be well as they hit the surface of the water. 'We planed along and it seemed quite normal,' he explained. 'Everyone relaxed, thinking that we had come down safely.'

Bevis continued: 'Suddenly I was shaken all over the place. There was a juddering and a hammering and then I was in the water. The plane's nose was up and I saw light and swam towards it and managed to crawl out on the wing.' At this point Bevis had seen one of his colleagues in difficulty in the water and had dived in to save him.

Squadron Leader Duncan Dobbie had been a member of the Air Ministry's Enquiry Team. They had carried out a thorough investigation. 'But,' he admitted, 'we are really no wiser as to the cause of the accident, which is quite an exceptional one for this type of aircraft.'

The plane, Dobbie said, had been well handled. The pilot was extremely competent, an above average flier. He had touched down at normal speed. The conditions in the landing area were suitable. There could be no suggestion of pilot error.

Dobbie then referred to another matter. 'Any suggestion of an obstruction in the sea can be discounted.'

But what about the aircraft itself? There was a story that loose nuts and bolts had been seen by observers at Eastbourne. Had a spar under one of the wings been broken prior to landing?

There was no evidence of anything like that, Dobbie said. 'The plane was both seaworthy and airworthy.

But a newspaper had mentioned the possibility of metal fatigue. Dobbie dismissed such an idea.

'Would you go so far as to say that these speculations about loose nuts and bolts and metal fatigue were quite irresponsible?' the coroner prompted.

'Yes, I would,' the squadron leader replied. 'Any loose nuts and bolts could be caused by towing. The plane was badly mutilated by beaching it.'

The salvaged tail end of the Sunderland is beached for inspection.

101

Further along the beach the wing section is brought ashore.

The coroner remarked that he wished he had known of these tales. He would have summoned the person responsible for them as a witness.

As it is, the reason for the dramatic end of the Sunderland flying boat off Eastbourne was never discovered. It remains simply a grim outcome for what ought to have been a day of untrammelled enjoyment.

A VIGOROUS ATLANTIC DEPRESSION

THE GREAT STORM, OCTOBER 16, 1987

THE greatest natural disaster that this country has suffered in over two and a half centuries occurred during the lifetime of most of the readers of this book. There have been storms enough since the Great Storm of 1703 – and make no mistake, that was a storm and a half with an estimated 8000 deaths, though most of them were at sea – but none of the other storms of this or the last century can match that which struck this country in the early hours of October 16, 1987. This was a storm which unleashed itself on Sussex with unbounded savagery. Many places south of a line from the Severn to the Wash suffered greatly but none so severely as Sussex and neighbouring Kent.

Though there had been a stiff breeze mounting to a strong wind throughout the evening, the storm did not hit the coast of Sussex until about two thirty in the morning. For the next three and a half hours, the wind rose and between lulls, reached recorded speeds of unusual strength. At Shoreham-by-Sea, it registered 85mph; at Crawley and Gatwick 99mph; at Eastbourne 104mph; and at Brighton 113mph. In the middle hours, from 3am until after 5am, it raged its furious worst across Sussex causing not only injury and loss of life, but a relentless devastation to the urban and rural landscape.

It is rare that we learn of evacuations in this country over so wide an area. Yet here, in the early, menacing hours when chimney pots fell, when trees were uprooted, when peeled-off roofs were bustled along the streets like wind-blown litter, people in their night clothes fled for their lives, in search of safety elsewhere. At Bexhill, where a penthouse was ripped away from a residential development, forty occupants were evacuated. Pensioners at Lancing were taken from their sheltered housing to the parish hall. Caravan parks at Rye Harbour and Selsey, the extreme east and west points of Sussex, were destroyed as their frightened owners made their escape. At Peacehaven, dangerously high up on a night such as this, and where the damage was perhaps the worst in the region, 200 caravans ended the night as matchwood.

The coast was so vulnerable. Windows were blown out of practically every shop front in Worthing and the elms, so long and so significant a feature of Brighton's Old Steine and the Royal Pavilion, were plucked effortlessly out of

At the Crumbles, this boat was blown across the road. Picture: Becketts

the ground. And all along the coast, where hundreds of fishing boats had been left drawn up on beaches ready for the next day's trip, or where pleasure craft had been lodged in anticipation of just a couple more weekends of sailing, the seaside roads were littered with wrecked craft which had been picked up and thrown disdainfully away with maximum force.

Anything of height was vulnerable. At St Leonards, the spire of St Luke's United Reformed Church was lifted from its tower and, after passing through the roof, deposited in a side aisle. Chichester Cathedral, where those who thought about it might have feared a repetition of 1861, lost no more than a finial which, after falling through the roof, broke a stained glass window. The more humble St Denys at Rotherfield lost its sixty-five foot spire, so long a landmark. At Newhaven, a towering container crane keeled over. At the Robert de Mortain pub at Hastings, a chimney stack came through the ceiling. An electricity pylon – not the only one of these to be blown down – crashed through the roof of a cottage at Horsted Keynes, mercifully sparing the owner. The windmill at Winchelsea was a victim of the storm. So, too, was Jill, consort to Jack, on the shoulder of the Downs at Clayton. The wind was so powerful here that her brakes failed to restrain the sweeps and they began to turn at a furious rate. The consequent friction set her on fire. It is one of the great tales of the storm of '87, the fire-fighting episode to save Jill. For against all the

This van was crushed by a tree in Willingdon Road, Eastbourne. Picture: Becketts

The force of the wind uprooted this tree, and with it a gravestone at Cradle Hill Cemetery, Seaford. Picture: Becketts

odds, a team from the windmill's preservation group made their way there – and if the journey up the hill was not epic, then it does deserve some kind of especially descriptive word because battling their way there required more than just physical strength – and, forming a human chain to the nearby cottage, they poured bucket after bucket of water on the flames. And succeeded. These people were true heroes.

And there were other stories, too. Jeremy Cottingham, a twenty-six-year old agricultural contractor, lay in his bed, planning perhaps the next night's stag party or more likely, his wedding on Saturday morning. Or, of course, he might have been asleep when the tree crashed through the roof of his caravan. Only the freezer, by the way it was positioned, saved him. And the wedding? That went ahead at Ripe church as planned, although only after Jeremy and

106

others cleared a way for the cars on the Golden Cross to Ripe road. But there was no stag party. Work on the clearance gave no time for such frivolity.

At Burgess Hill, Antony Bryant, nine, was in bed when the chimney fell through the ceiling. The debris filled the room waist high. Remarkably, he was untouched. His twelve-year-old brother, David, was fortunate, too. When the storm began, he had gone into Antony's room, thinking about spending the night there in the spare bed but then he decided to return to his own bedroom. In the spare bed, he would have been killed, crushed by the roof.

The Tinklers, Alan and Julie, also from Burgess Hill, escaped narrowly when wardrobes in their bedroom fell down after a tree branch came through the ceiling. Inches either way and their lives would have been lost.

At the height of the storm, on his way to carry out emergency electrical work, Martin Jones's car was hit by a tree. He was considerably shaken but not injured. He abandoned the car and took shelter in a telephone box. Strangely, the line was intact and he was able to phone his wife at Heathfield. He was probably surprised in the succeeding days to see newspaper photographs of telephone boxes which had been moved by the power of the wind.

One Haywards Heath woman went from her house with relatives just before a tree came through the roof and on to the chair she had been sitting in only a short time before. Georgina Wells, sixty-seven, from the same town, was struck by a tree which came through her ceiling. After five days, she died in hospital.

There were other deaths, too. At Hove a mother of two was killed when the chimney stack came through her ceiling. A Rottingdean man went out to his garage to prevent the doors being torn off. The effort brought on a fatal heart attack. And forty-nine-year old Jimmy Read, working with other fishermen to drag the boats at Hastings higher up the beach, was killed when the roof of a winch hut hit him. Also in Hastings, the glass roof of the Queen's Hotel fell into the foyer. After that, a chimney stack fell through four floors and a male

A pile of timber is all that was left of a barn at Merryweathers Farm, Chelsham Lane, Herstmonceux. Picture: Becketts

The wrecked showroom at Blackboys Service Station. Picture: Becketts

guest was killed. So while some escaped and others died, while some rescued windmills and others were evacuated, the storm raged.

Off came a Tudor chimney at Glynde and down came a two-ton minaret, right through the roof of Brighton's Royal Pavilion, down into the Music Room where it severely damaged a new carpet valued at £86,000. The offending stone was removed after three hours' struggle by a team of fifteen men. Tideway School at Newhaven was ripped apart, with damage estimated at £500,000. Pulborough Village Hall lost its gable end – nor was it the only building to suffer in this fashion: it was a night for gable ends. And for roofs, too, such as the one belonging to the Ordes of Seaford whose roof not only was tugged off but went careering down the road, coming to rest only after it had hit two cars and a caravan.

There is a recklessness in the way the wind treated whatever stood in its way. Perhaps it could be likened to the unruly infant of some fairy tale giant for things were tossed about at random and what had seemed only hours before to be fixtures of permanence and constancy, were now callously discarded. The flint barn at Edburton and that at Stream Farm at Chiddingly, after centuries of the fiercest winds, at last met their match and were unceremoniously pushed over. If such as these could not withstand this insolent force, it is no wonder that a tree fell across twenty cars at East Sussex Police

108

Headquarters in Lewes; no wonder that seventeen aircraft at Shoreham Airport were flipped over like children's toys on to their backs and sides; no wonder that buildings inland as well as on the sea's edge were stained with the shingle, sand and salt that had been hurled at them. It was the same heedless child who flicked over high-sided vehicles and who with a sweep of a hand, flattened great woodlands and who pushed over churchyard trees so that, as at Ninfield, they caused the very gravestones to tilt at the most extreme angles.

A storm? Is that all it was? Surely it qualified for a grander description than that. This was an occurrence that changed the shape, altered the balance of our countryside. Whole woodlands disappeared so that a trip out into the country-side now reveals an entirely new landscape. The copses that graced hilltops, the coverts that sloped across the crowns of meadows, the great parklands, the vast plantations which were recognised features of Sussex were simply tugged out, scattered, so that great trees which had seemed so permanent lay like dis-carded matchsticks across the face of the land. This was the storm that so man-gled Chanctonbury Ring, that great landmark to landsmen and seamen alike, that two thirds of its 40ft beeches, planted more than 200 years earlier, were destroyed. The same storm laid 300 trees across the railway line from Tunbridge Wells to Battle, a distance of no more than thirty miles, and made impassable long stretches of every other line. The statistics of fallen trees, like most of the statistics relating to that day of destruction, are mind-numbing, impossible totally to absorb. Nevertheless, here are some to help us fathom the extent of the devastation.

Probably fifteen million trees in England were destroyed. Four or five mil-lion of these were lost in Sussex. Nymans at Handcross lost twenty out of twenty-eight Champions, trees which by their height or girth were larger than any others of their kind. The largest monkey puzzle tree in the country was destroyed here, too.

At Wakehurst, the rural wing of the Royal Botanical Society, half of the important trees were blown down. The National Trust property at Standen was able some months later to sell 1,500 tons of beech to Turkey. At Sheffield Park huge and venerable trees, planted over 200 years earlier by Capability Brown, fell to earth. And in another of Brown's masterworks, the Pleasure Garden at Petworth, sweet chestnuts, plane trees and limes were cast down. That the trees this year were in full leaf and that the ground was soft after seriously heavy rains contributed to these losses. Stanmer Woods on the outskirts of Brighton lost 200 acres of woodland. The damage to Eastbourne's trees may serve as an illustration of how towns were affected. Here, 500 street, 700 woodland and 380 parkland trees were destroyed. At Pound Hill, Crawley, a magnificent walk of trees in Worth Park Avenue was sadly reduced. On the

Cars were almost buried by rubble in Southfields Road, Eastbourne, and here looters added to the misery by stealing from the wrecked vehicles. Picture: Becketts

morning after, the broad road to the station was impassable as the great trees lay across it every few yards. Easthill Park in Hastings lost seventy per cent of its trees. And the loss of trees, like the loss of anything of seeming permanence, is profoundly affecting. The destruction of the centuries-old Cedar of Lebanon in Holy Cross churchyard, Uckfield, was more deeply felt than the loss of the church roof.

Sussex experienced a dramatic and cruel transformation. After the storm, in very many places, they were no longer recognisable.

In the height of the storm, when electricity had broken down in so many parts of the region and communication by telephone was all but impossible, when the stretched emergency services were at their heroic best, at the other end of the scale the looters were out, foraging like rats, finding their way through shattered windows of major stores, lit only by the off-on of their burglar alarms. Videos, CDs, stereo units and thousands of other items were stolen from Debenhams at Eastbourne, from the Army and Navy Stores at Hove, and from so many other hard-hit towns – Worthing, Brighton, Bognor among them – all too hard pressed to deal with that kind of civil disorder on such a night.

The story became repetitive. From town to town, village to village, the scene was repeated over the dramatic three or four hours. And then at about six o'clock, the wind abated and gradually people emerged to view their altered world. The clearing up began. It was a mammoth task. And an expensive one. And a task that was not easily completed. Roads had to be cleared and whilst major roads were negotiable within a couple of days, others were less quickly opened up. One old couple living near Petworth finally had the trees to their isolated cottage cut away nine days after the storm.

Electricity had to be restored and some parts of Sussex had no supply for up to a fortnight. At Balcombe, villagers took their Christmas dinners from their freezers and cooked them on portable stoves. For a week, the Red Cross provided cooked lunches for forty in Ditchling Village Hall. It was all so reminiscent of earlier and even harder times when during the war neighbours helped each other. And it was especially hard for those who did not return to their devastated homes for months. Worse again for those whose houses had to be demolished, so seriously had they been damaged.

They say it was not a hurricane. At least the Met Office would not dignify it with such a name. In their reckoning it was simply 'a vigorous mid-latitude depression which intensified abruptly somewhere near the Bay of Biscay'. A hurricane, they say, is Force 12 with an average wind speed, measured over ten minutes, of seventy-three miles an hour. Though there were gusts well in excess of that they were not of sufficient duration according to the experts. Yet

Thirty people were left homeless when the hurricane-force winds struck this Newhaven mobile home park. Picture: Becketts

Shoreham claimed that it measured a ten-minute spell during which time wind speed averaged eighty-five miles an hour and did not fall below seventy-three. But that whole argument is in the past. And it was a mighty storm, call it what we will.

Most important is that the Met Office failed to forecast the great storm of 1987. And there are reasons for this which are not difficult to accept. Briefly, they had sparse information as they had only one weather ship in the Bay of Biscay. Further, the seven-year-old computer at Bracknell did not produce specific enough information for the forecasters. BBC weatherman, Michael Fish, an Eastbourne resident, will always have the unjust reputation as the man who said there was no hurricane on the way. He did, after all, warn of very strong winds though that element of his forecast has been forgotten.

The great storm of 1987 was indeed a disaster. It took the lives of half a dozen unsuspecting people who had retired to bed in the normality of an autumn evening. And it had, in the space of a few hours, changed so much in the county that was familiar and that had seemed to be for all time. Douglas

It was a similar scene at a caravan park in Seaford where this luxury mobile home collapsed like a pack of cards.. Picture: Becketts

Hurd, Home Secretary at the time, referred to it as 'the most widespread night of disaster in south-east England since 1945'. And few will gainsay that. Just as few who lived through it will ever forget it.

A PHOENIX RISEN

THE FIRE AT UPPARK, AUGUST 30, 1989

UPPARK, a dozen or so miles north of Chichester, is one of The National Trust's most popular houses. It welcomes well over 30,000 visitors each year. On any fine day in summer it is certain of a good crowd. By mid-afternoon on August 30, 1989, for instance, nearly 300 people had already passed through the house and others were queuing for entry at the portico entrance on the north side of the building.

It was one of those diamond-bright downland days, just the flimsiest net of cloud in a deep blue sky. Although the breeze from the south-west toned down some of the sun's heat, visitors strolled in the grounds, sat on the grass, the men jacketless, the women in summery clothes. They gazed at the mellow three-hundred-year-old brickwork of the house, its neat proportions, its regularity. Or perhaps they looked towards the south where the downs, which come almost to the very walls of Uppark, fall away. In the distance on clear days there are glimpses of the Channel, the Solent, the Isle of Wight. It is impossible to look in any direction and not be uplifted.

Uppark, that especial favourite of visitors, has two particular features which bring them back time and again. In addition, of course, to its wind-washed, sun-drenched site, it has the virtue of compactness. It is in fact a quite small house: a visit does not involve exhausting footslogging. Unlike many great houses, it does not overwhelm those who visit. And after a second or third visit it is small enough to be remembered, liked, as a familiar, as a friend almost.

And then, there is its interior, stocked with all the elegance, the restrained artistry of the late seventeenth and eighteenth centuries. Uppark owes much to its owners of those days, the people who built and then furnished it. It owes much also to those who followed on, who retained this example of exquisite taste.

No-one has described more clearly than Adam Nicolson exactly how the house revealed itself. 'Throughout all the tides of Victorian, Edwardian and twentieth century fashion, almost nothing has changed at Uppark,' Nicolson writes. 'It was kept as it was, glamorous but the glamour fading, curtains and bed-hangings repaired not replaced, paintings and pierglasses remaining where

114

Uppark today, virtually indistinguishable from the house destroyed by fire.

the people who had first bought them had hung them, wallpaper faded but unstripped, gilt unregilded, tables and chairs unaltered, vases, carpets, sofas, bookcases, candle-sticks, sconces and clocks – all this untouched and unmoved.'

It was not, of course, the neglect of a Miss Havisham: rather it was the aristocratic or upper middle-class way of understated perfection.

Visit Uppark and you visit the topmost layer of eighteenth century elegance with not the slightest hint of vulgarity or over-indulgence. What a tribute to its founder, Forde Grey, later Earl of Tankerville. Rascal, traitor, turncoat, he was all of these. Strange that so cynical a man in so cynical a time should build this uncomplicated house. It has no surprises; its very shape, its clean lines, bespeak honesty, straightforwardness.

Matthew Fetherstonhaugh, his successor in 1746, steps out of a fairy tale. He is instructed to leave his home in Northumberland to seek a wife and an estate. If he can succeed in this, he will inherit a vast fortune from a wealthy relative in the South of England. He completes his task with ease; he marries the daughter of a wealthy merchant and takes on Uppark. The vast fortune is his and the couple live happily ever after. They make improvements; they tour in Europe and ship home all the treasures they can find.

Their son, Harry, is a scapegrace, a gambler, a close friend of the Prince Regent. All society beats its way to Uppark, so extravagant are his parties. Wellington visits, so does Nelson whose lover-to-be, Emma (later Lady Hamilton), is Harry's mistress. Some say that she danced on the dining table for the guests. Naked, they say.

But Harry, aged seventy, settles down, marries his dairy maid, fifty years his junior, and after his death, many years later, she and her sister manage the house, not changing it. The sister does not die until 1895 yet she has links back to the previous century. It is a long chain.

After The National Trust bought the house in 1954, no efforts were made to change Uppark. What the visitors were seeing on August 30, 1989 would have been recognisable to Forde Grey, to Matthew Fetherstonhaugh and to each of the others who in earlier times had created the house. In turn, the present owners, the Meade-Fetherstonhaughs, would not have found the house of two and three hundred years ago, much less that of the nineteenth century, especially strange.

When the fire alarm first sounded shortly after 3.30pm many of the visitors in the house assumed that they were either hearing a routine alarm test or participating in a fire practice. Or perhaps, they thought, someone had pressed a button in error. Nevertheless, they allowed themselves to be ushered out of the house. As they passed along the ground floor, through the dining room, stone hall, saloon, red drawing room and tapestry room, there was no hint of fire, no whiff of smoke.

Once on the lawns, they joined others who stared up at the pediment on the house's south face. Minutes earlier there had been the faintest wisps of smoke up there and the builders, who had been working on the roof for the past year, and who had been scheduled to finish their work the following day, had scrambled up on to the scaffolding with fire extinguishers. Their attempts to contain the fire were useless. By now the flames were clearly visible, dancing along the roof and spreading towards the south-east corner of the house.

Fortunately – and this was to prove significant – fire drill routines were firmly established at Uppark. The National Trust had always been aware of its treasures. Nevertheless, at this early stage, no-one suspected how serious this fire was to be.

The first fire engines arrived from Petersfield very quickly, followed by others from Midhurst and later, yet others from Chichester. By 4.30pm there were twenty engines on site and others were sent for. Eventually, twenty-seven fire engines and one hundred and fifty firemen tackled the blaze that was very obviously gaining control.

The fire was located at first in the roof space. Here, the first phase of the battle was fought. The intense heat was already melting the lead on the roof and firemen were struggling to maintain a foothold.

Immediately below, on the first floor, Brian Bloomfield, the administrator at Uppark and Brian Smith, the custodian, had gathered a team of stewards. They feared for the Meade-Fetherstonhaugh's family quarters and began to take out their possessions from their private drawing room. Already water from the hoses was seeping through the ceiling and it was clearly in danger of falling. The rescuers set about removing furniture, paintings, porcelain and a variety of other precious items to another room on the same floor. They were completely unaware of the progress the fire above them was to make.

On the ground floor, members of the Meade-Fetherstonhaugh family had themselves gathered some helpers together. Harriet Corsart and Emma Goad, with younger members of the family, were joined by stewards and members of the public. Together they carried out more furniture, more paintings, and a great number of other items from the Tapestry Room. These were brought on to the lawn and from there carried by others to the tea room and the stables.

Meanwhile, the firemen were in retreat from the attic, thrown back by the heat and by the vanishing floorboards on which they stood. Now, the ceilings below them were in increasing danger of collapse.

As their husbands were struggling to save the many valuable items on the first floor, Joan Bloomfield and Jan Smith were at work in the Little Parlour, where the fire's hot breath would eventually melt the chandelier. From there and from an adjoining room, helped by others, they lugged out cupboards, chairs, sofas, pictures.

By now the roof blazed unimpeded and thick clouds of smoke billowed into the summer sky. Thousands of gallons of water were having little effect. The first floor was being overtaken by fire.

Down below, tapestries were torn down from walls; curtains were yanked away from rails; Wilton carpets were hurriedly rolled and carried out on the shoulders of teams of eight. Such items, sometimes soaked through and made even heavier by the water from the firemen's appliances, were flung with little ceremony on to the lawns.

By five o'clock the first floor had to be abandoned. The fire, which had penetrated the ceiling, had also insinuated itself into the gap between the brickwork of the outer wall and the oak panelling of several of the rooms. Now it raged unrestrained, consuming as it went bleached white floors, gently fading textiles, bell pulls, ornate gilt mirrors, chintz furnishings, and a range of items scarcely moved since their arrival at the house 300 years earlier. Within an hour they were lost.

Outside, now fighting from the high platform of a tall hydraulic crane, the

117

firemen hosed down the lost roof, the lost attic, the lost first floor. Others at ground level aimed their hoses at the flames now visible through the first-floor windows. But there was concern that the supply of water was running low. Each engine's supply of 400 gallons was nearly empty; an underground spring was tapped and dried up; the pool in which only an hour or so earlier members of the family had been swimming was almost used up. Yet the fire showed no signs of abating.

Now that the fire brigade and the other rescuers were confined to the ground floor every effort was directed at recovering whatever was movable from that area. Out came flamboyant mirrors; the great paintings, works of Canaletto, of Giordano, of Batoni; out came more curtains, bed hangings, tapestries; whatever could be manhandled in the furnace, in the overpowering dense smoke, in the roar and crackle of the flames, in the raining down of loosened bricks, of spars, beams, tumbling from above.

In the Staircase Hall more pictures were taken down, but once more the fire fighters were forced to retreat when the huge stucco ceiling ornament above the stairwell crashed down two floors and when the staircase itself, undermined, crashed down.

As the fire tore on according to its will, the ceiling of the Stone Hall came down. A Gothic style lantern was twisted by the heat beyond recognition. A beam fell on to two Florentine scagliola tables. These, decorated with classical landscapes in coloured plaster, had been, like so many other items in the house, rare trophies from the Grand Tour. The top of one of the tables was shattered; the gilt wood legs of the other were broken.

Now, desperate to save as much as possible, the firemen threw out what they could. Out through the doors, out through the windows, came whatever could be lifted, thrown out regardless almost of consequences.

After five o'clock, fire engines, swimming pool and spring had run dry. A chain of fire engines pumped water uphill to the site from the main at South Harting village a mile away. Later a private lake, recently stocked with fish, was to be used as a source until it ran dry. Ultimately, throughout the night two water-carriers, each with a capacity of 5,000 gallons, and six engines were to shuttle water from several miles away.

The fire was not overcome until after dawn the following day, when chimney stacks had tumbled, when every ceiling had fallen, when oak panelling and oak floors had been destroyed. With the light, the exhausted men and women who had fought so gamely for fifteen hours were able to ascertain the extent of the damage. Gone was the roof; gone the two upper floors. It was a shell they were left with, open to the sky. Here and there little spurts of fire started up for the last time. Thick ashy sludge, two feet deep, covered the

118

ground floor. It was a scene of the most acute desolation. Uppark, that delightful house, so firm a favourite, seemed to have ended its days. This was perhaps The National Trust's most serious loss, its worst fire.

So many grand houses have been seriously damaged or lost as a result of fire in recent years. In 1984 Heveringham Hall in Suffolk was a casualty and two years later, Hampton Court. Braidwood Castle in Strathclyde was another in 1988. And there are many other examples. Certainly, the hurt felt by those concerned is deep. After Coleshill in Wiltshire was burnt in 1953, so great was the demoralisation that it was never rebuilt and even its shell was demolished. Elizabethan Rushbrooke, Jacobean Surrenden Deering, Caroline Uffington, Palladian Foot's Cray, neo-classical Roseneath are all of them just ruins.

'Demolish it,' David Martin, a Portsmouth MP advised. 'It was only built by Restoration yuppies,' he said. 'Return the site to nature,' he proclaimed, providing further evidence that elevation to Parliament is no guarantee of either sense or sensibility.

Yet today the house stands, reconstituted. It is a phoenix risen. It is a triumph of the architects and archaeological conservators, of highly skilled craftsmen, of workers in wood, metal, plaster, glass, of weavers and embroiderers. The story, not to be told here, is a counterbalance to the disaster of the fire. After five years the house was again opened. Of course, the debate has raged. Is it the same house or is it not? Is it a repair, a restoration, a re-creation? Is it a copy? Is it a fake? Whatever it may be, it is a remarkable piece of work and the new cannot always be distinguished from the old.

And the cause of the fire?

Two workmen who had been using blowtorches on the lead roof had gone off for a tea-break. Perhaps they had been doing that over the past year when working on the roof. Whether they had or not, when they returned they were confronted by the first indications of the fire. Of course, they had broken the rules. The roof should not have been left within fifteen minutes of using the torches, to allow the lead to cool down. But working practices are too often imperfect and sometimes the results are as they were at Uppark.

Some even say that it could have been worse, that it would have been so had the central hall and staircase not acted as a giant chimney which allowed the fire to roar inwardly and not scorch the outside of the building.

A small mercy, it might be said.

SOURCES

MAGAZINES:
Sussex County Magazine, Vol 12
Ripping Panel, December 1917
Royal Sanitary Institution Journal, 1952
Chichester Cathedral Journal, 1961
Gazette Magazine, April 1975
Patrol, September 1977
Sussex History, No 8 1984
Sussex History, No 24 1987
Wingspan No 51, March 1989

NEWSPAPERS:
Hastings Observer; Brighton Gazette; Brighton Guardian; Brighton Herald; Eastbourne Herald; Evening Argus; Observer and West Sussex Recorder; Sussex Daily News; Sussex Express; Sussex Weekly Advertiser; West Sussex Gazette; The Times.

SUSSEX ARCHAEOLOGICAL COLLECTION:
Volumes vii; xiv; xvii; lxiv.

PERSONAL ACCOUNTS:
Blackman, Herbert, *The Story of Battle Gunpowder Mills,* 1918
Thompson, William, *The Lewes Avalanche,* c1870

GENERAL READING:
Baker, Michael HC, *London to Brighton,* 1989
Bishop, JG *The Brighton Chain Pier* ,1896
Clunn, Harold, *Famous South Coast Pleasure Resorts,* 1929
Corlette, Herbert, *The Cathedral Church of Chichester,* 1901
Guilmant, Aylwin, *Bygone Battle,* 1983
Hill, George, *Hurricane Force,* 1988
Horsfield, Thomas, *A History of Sussex,* 1835
Hutchinson, Geoff, *The Mary Stanford Disaster,* 1984
Lucey, Beryl, *Twenty Centuries in Sedlescombe,* 1978
Musgrave, Clifford, *Life in Brighton,* 1970
Nairn and Pevsner, *Sussex,* 1965
Nicolson, Adam, *The Fire at Uppark,* 1990
Ogley, Bob, *The Sussex Weather Book,* 1991
Swinfen and Arscott, *Hidden Sussex Day by Day,* 1987
Wynter, WR, *Old Seaford,* 1922

I am grateful to Tony Payne, chairman of Peacehaven History Society, who most generously permitted me to use his unpublished research material on the 1809 convoy disaster; to Brian Allchorn of Eastbourne for the photographs of the Sunderland flying boat; to the RNLI for photographs relating to the Rye lifeboat disaster, and to Beckett Newspapers for photographs of the 1987 hurricane.